"Getting your essential greens everyday 'on the go' to alkalize your body has never been easier than with the many delicious options that The Juice Truck offers. Now we get to know their tasty secrets for successful cleansing with juices and for creating our very own plant-based meals with their crowd pleasing recipes! I could eat these amazing yummy dishes morning, noon and night and I probably will!"

JULIE COVE, bestselling author of *Eat Better, Live Better, Feel Better*

"Who better to learn from about juicing, smoothies and the plant-based lifestyle than Canada's cold-pressed juice pioneers? . . . This book can help kick-start a healthy lifestyle and perhaps even motivate readers to pursue their dreams, as Zach and Ryan have done so successfully."

ERIN IRELAND, food reporter and editor of itstodiefor.ca

"What you hold in your hands is not only an excellent resource for vibrant juice and smoothie recipes; it's a useful guide equipping you with the tools you need to start creating your own colorful elixirs. . . . If you are looking for more energy and nutrition in your life via delicious drink recipes: look no further, you've hit gold with this one."

EMILY von EUW, bestselling cookbook author and blogger behind *This Rawsome Vegan Life*

"Juicing as a trend seems to be everywhere now, but for Zach and Ryan, The Juice Truck began many years ago, inspired by their months of travel around India and Nepal. They drew on local customs and ancient knowledge of nutrition and medicines found naturally in plants. This book takes juicing farther than a fad: they speak of a way to truly nourish yourself as a way of life—physically, spiritually, holistically, and most importantly, in my opinion, deliciously."

JACKIE KAI ELLIS, owner of Beaucoup Bakery & Café

"Eating well is not about restriction and sacrifice . . . it's about joyfully feeding your body what it needs to feel its best. The recipes in this book are as joyful, vibrant and yummy as it gets. The more you enjoy these nutrient-dense treats in your daily life, the better you will feel. No matter where you are with your eating habits, *The Juice Truck* makes it so easy to put more plants on your plate."

DESIREE NIELSEN RD, Host of *Urban Vegetarian* and author of *Un-Junk Your Diet*

THE JUICE TRUCK

By founders of The Juice Truck
ZACH BERMAN AND RYAN SLATER

with health coach Colin Medhurst

appetite
by RANDOM HOUSE

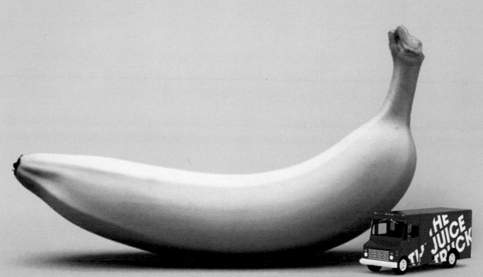

This book is dedicated to Eden Elizabeth,
her life, the amazing message she shared,
and her spirit that inspired so many
in her short time on this earth.

CONTENTS

THE INTRO

THE JUICE ON JUICING

HOW TO START A JUICE BUSINESS

Travel does many things to you. Committing to the open path, to the adventure of the unknown, liberates your mind and opens up possibilities and opportunities to go anywhere. Our travels took us to the Himalayas and Nepal, and that is where our journey into the juicing world began.

My childhood friend Ryan Slater and I had both recently graduated from university. After five years of studying urban planning and visual art, where we planned future cities and dreamed up nature scenes, we were hungry for adventure. We decided to save up and take off to Nepal, a dream destination bursting with mysticism, magic, and mountains.

In the fall of 2009, we were on the yak trail, ready for Himalayan peaks and thrills. Early into our first trek, we got snowed in at a small mountain town called Manang, on our way around the Annapurna circuit. As we waited for the storm to pass, we noticed the locals drinking a vibrant orange drink. We learned that this drink was made from sea-buckthorn berries. The sea-buckthorn produces a small, tart berry. It grows at high altitudes and has a unique capacity to withstand adverse conditions. Its berry, packed with essential omegas, iron, potassium, calcium, and vitamins, gave the isolated local community nutrients their otherwise starchy potato- and rice-based diet lacked.

From that moment on, our trip revolved around seeking out the local health secrets and remedies. Sea-buckthorn and shilajit in Nepal; moringa leaf powder, ashwagandha and turmeric in India; and the best king coconuts we've ever tasted in Sri Lanka. We even met a guy in New Delhi who was somehow able to juice bananas (we're still not sure how that works). Every day, we would frequent the local juice stand in whatever city we found ourselves exploring. Over and over again, these street communities of juicers greeted us juice-obsessed foreigners with eager smiles and insanely delicious locally made juices.

We arrived back in Vancouver, British Columbia, in the fall of 2010 with juice fresh on our minds. Since we had probably numbed our response to fear by going on dangerous Himalayan hikes, rafting down glacier rivers, and riding motorcycles throughout the bustling roads of India, the idea of starting a business didn't seem the least bit scary. We like to say we brought a nice combination of naïveté and positivity into launching our business.

We spent the next six months researching, blending, and pressing everything possible in my parents' kitchen. Our experimentation yielded recipes that worked and recipes that definitely did not work. We stubbornly tried for weeks to come up with a great durian recipe, but never quite got there. (Anyone who's tried this popular but foul-smelling South Asian fruit will understand the challenge.) We brought in focus groups—exercise fanatics to less active people, young to old, male and female—to learn what recipes to launch with. All the while, we were trying to learn how to cold-press juice fresh to order, something no other cold-pressed juice bar had done at the time (we are still one of the only juice bars in the world to offer this). Once we figured out the menu, our next mountain to climb was financing. We quickly learned that enthusiasm wasn't enough. Back to Zach's parents' place, this time with piles of scrap paper and blue-sky ideas, to figure out the costing and the logistics of sustaining a business. About ten months had passed from when we decided to enter the juicing world full-time, at the age of twenty-four, with a shoestring backpackers' budget. We were ready to go.

In the summer of 2011, we launched the Juice Truck, Canada's first cold-pressed juice bar, in the form of a watermelon-pink mobile food truck. We wanted to bring that same street-side accessibility and friendliness that inspired us throughout our travels back home to Vancouver. Driven by community and health and wellness for the masses, the Juice Truck has become a fixture in Vancouver.

As our business grew, we wanted to keep developing our own understanding of nutrition and plant-based living. In 2012, we started working with our childhood friend Eden MacDonald and her husband Colin Medhurst, the founders of Feed Life, on our next chapter in the juicing world: the Juice Cleanse, a home and office delivery program.

In 2011, Colin and a group of firefighters traveled to Sri Lanka to help Eden finish building a nutrition center, part of a project by a nonprofit built and funded by Eden. AIM International Aid Society provides nutrition and health care for children in Sri Lanka. After returning home from the trip, Colin and Eden launched their own health and wellness business, Feed Life, where they work in a private practice in Vancouver teaching nutrition and culinary workshops. Founded on a personal passion for cancer prevention and healing, Feed Life's mission is to show how nourishing and delicious it can be to eat whole, plant-based foods. At twenty-five, Eden turned to food as a way to revitalize her body after a cancer diagnosis. Realizing the lack of quality information about natural healing, Eden and Colin created in-person and online classes in holistic health and wellness. Their company has reached thousands of people through their workshops promoting a plant-based, nutrient-dense whole-food diet, mindfulness practices, and clean living.

Inspired by the depth of knowledge, experience, and passion we saw in Feed Life, we began collaborating on one health endeavor after another together. It began with the Juice Cleanse, and then moved to menu development and consultation. We continue to work with Feed Life to expand and evolve our plant-powered business, the Juice Truck.

WHY JUICE?

Juice has gotten big in the last few years. It's hard to miss on your daily feeds on Instagram and Facebook, celebrities are endorsing it and investing in it, and juice bars are popping up all over the country at the same speed as coffee bars.

Our love affair with juice began during our travels, when we started seeking out the local juice stand to jump-start our day with some pressed greens. This wasn't the pasteurized, prepackaged OJ and fruit mixes we grew up with; this was fresh pressed and made with whole fruit and vegetables. Once we added juice to our morning routine, we discovered each day we felt more amazing than the last. It was a simple change in our habits and yet the effect on our bodies was staggering. That was it—we were hooked. And best of all, it was so easy to fit into our hectic schedule of traveling that implementing it at home would be a breeze.

No matter what the day brings, including juice in our daily ritual keeps us feeling grounded, energized, and healthy. Putting a clear focus on our health first thing kick-starts a positive and purpose-driven day. Healthy habits make for healthy lives, and fresh juice provides minerals, vitamins, carbohydrates, proteins, and more. A juice a day can strengthen your immune system, increase your energy, improve your skin, build stronger bones, soothe your nerves, stimulate your brain, and reduce the risk of many diseases. Plus, with the right recipes it's delicious, refreshing, and hydrating, which is every bit as important. Especially the delicious part.

Fresh juice is a key ingredient to an active lifestyle, a catalyst for new healthier habits, and a go-to for health seekers. It's the easiest way to get your daily dose of nutrients and enzymes in one go and to make sure you get the recommended amount of fruit and vegetables in your diet. It's a fast and easy way for your body to efficiently absorb immune-boosting nutrients naturally found in fresh fruit and vegetables—juicing liberates enzymes and nutrients whose absorption is sometimes blocked by the fiber of whole fruit and vegetables.

JUICE VERSUS SMOOTHIES

Juicing versus blending: it sounds like a great rivalry, but it's more like a friendship. They go together like kale and spinach, or almond butter and . . . well, everything goes with almond butter. You get the point—they're a great team.

First, let's be clear with what we mean by juice. We are talking about the fresh-pressed kind, as in it was a whole vegetable or fruit moments before it was a cup full of liquid ready for you to drink. If it's pasteurized, concentrated, heat treated, or lasts on the shelf for longer than a week, it's not the kind of juice that we promote drinking. Juicing removes most of the pulpy insoluble fiber, essentially leaving you with a cup of nutrient-rich water. Though fiber has its place in our diets, removing most of it from your juice expedites nutrient absorption. If you're not having a meal or a snack with your juice, add some of the pulp back so that you get the fiber your body needs. Think of juicing as the fast lane for phytochemicals, minerals, antioxidants, and vitamins to make their way through your body.

Smoothies are more like a meal in comparison to their juicy counterpart. Blending retains all of the fiber as the blender pulverizes, mashes, and mixes all of the fruits, vegetables, nuts, and liquids into a rich, robust, calorically dense, nutrition-packed smoothie. Since smoothies are blended, your stomach interprets them as a partially pre-digested meal, and the nutrients are easily digested. The fiber aids in digestion and helps regulate blood glucose levels by slowing down the absorption of sugar. The best thing about smoothies is you can soup them up with superfoods and medicinal foods, adding the seeds, powders, and herbs of your choice. There are only so many ingredients you can juice, but with smoothies the sky's the limit. It's fun to play alchemist and experiment with ingredients. It's also great for kids—you can sneak greens in and mask the flavor with frozen berries.

So as we said, it's not really a competition. We love juice *and* smoothies. We recommend keeping both predominantly vegetable based to avoid unnecessary sugar intake, which can cause your insulin to spike. Juices and smoothies are both celebrated in a healthy lifestyle. And since juice is good any time of day and smoothies are more of a meal replacement, you can have your juice and eat it too. When you're deciding which to make, just do what works best for your schedule. You're more likely to make a habit out of whichever is convenient, and in the end, the more juice and the more smoothies you consume, the more your body is going to thank you. And if you want to turn this friendship into a marriage, or make what we like to call a super smoothie, use the fresh-pressed juice as the liquid base for your smoothie.

THE JUICE ON THIS BOOK

This book breaks down the basics of what juices, smoothies, and a plant-based diet can do for you. We'll tell you how to get started right in the comfort of your own home. Whether your goal is simply to make drinking green juice and smoothies part of your daily routine, or you're looking to get into juice cleansing and plant-based foods in a bigger way, this book is your guide to learning the power of fruit and vegetables and the changes they can make to your everyday life.

Busy schedules, tight budgets, and even a fear of the kitchen can get in the way of your health goals. It's easy to make the goal of healthy eating seem too complicated to bother with. But juicing is an easy way to complement an active, busy life with the nutrients that your body craves. We'll help you choose the right juicer or blender and stock the best ingredients in your kitchen, and then we'll set you up with mouthwatering, health-positive recipes that will make juicing an easy and fun part of your daily routine.

Welcome to your journey into the juice world! This book is just the start. Each ingredient has its own benefits. As you experiment, you'll discover what resonates with you, and you'll learn to adapt to new demands as your body's needs change. Hippocrates said, "Let food be thy medicine and medicine be thy food." Juicing can be a part of that medicine, and can keep you healthy from the inside out.

WELCOME TO YOUR JOURNEY INTO THE JUICE WORLD!

A LOOSE HISTORY OF JUICING

Though there are no historical records, experts hypothesize that even our cave-dwelling ancestors would smash fruits and drink the leftover liquids. Juicing has come a long way since its conjectured origins. Here is the road from caveman to cold pressed.

8000 BCE
Grape pits dated to 8000 BCE are considered to be early evidence of juice production.

1700 BCE
Ancient Greeks believe pomegranate juice is an aphrodisiac and claim it as a love potion.

1000 BCE
The earliest documented lemonade is discovered in Egypt, dating to around 1000 BCE.

150 BCE
The earliest documentation of humans making juice for health benefits is found in the dead sea scrolls from 150 BCE to 70 CE. The scrolls mention a "pounded mash of pomegranate and fig" resulting in "profound strength."

500 CE
From 500CE to 1500 CE suggestions of juicing appear from Peru, Korea, and Japan. Many cultures used ground-up plants and applied them externally and internally for health benefits.

1867
James Lind connected citrus fruits to the prevention of scurvy in the eighteenth century. This led to the Merchant Shipping Act of 1867, which requires all ocean-bound British ships to carry citrus juice on board.

1910
Juice pasteurization is developed and the National Rail starts to offer breakfast orange juice.

1920
Max Gerson, a German scientist, develops therapy combining a plant-based diet and raw juices. This therapy, called Gerson therapy, is still practiced today.

1936
The book *Raw Vegetable Juices* is published in 1936 by Dr. Norman Walker. The Norwalk juicer was a result of this book and became the world's first household juicer. After seventy years of studying, Dr. Walker developed a philosophy: the best way to nutritional health was with a diet consisting mostly of raw food and juices. He coined the term "Living Food."

1954

The Champion Juicer, the world's first masticating juicer, is invented.

1970

Jack Lalanne, an American fitness and nutritional expert, comes onto the scene in the 1970s and is named the "the godfather of fitness." Lalanne promotes the power of juicing and the health benefits from fresh, unprocessed foods. He coined the saying, "That's the power of the juice!"

1971

Harry Nilsson releases the song "Coconut" in 1971, popularizing the saying, "Put the lime in the coconut!" Coconuts and limes have been together ever since.

1975

Beverly Hills Juice launches in 1975. The first juice bar to use the Norwalk to make cold-pressed juices, almost thirty years before any other juice bar.

1989

Jay Kordich, a pioneer in juicing and nutritional health, appears for the first time on TV on a juicing infomercial.

1993

The Green Power Juicer is invented in Korea. The twin gear extraction process was based on the idea of using a mortar-and-pestle action to press out the juice without losing nutrients or enzymes from high-speed blades or heat and friction.

Snoop Dogg writes the song "Gin and Juice" in 1993. This led to juice and alcohol entering a time of celebrated union.

2000

Blue Print Cleanse launches in the early 2000s; the first of the contemporary cold-pressed juice, kick starting a modern juicing movement. In 2010 Joe Cross from Australia produced a documentary called *Fat, Sick and Nearly Dead*, focusing on a sixty-day juice cleanse. The documentary goes viral and kicks off an international juicing craze.

2009

Zach Berman and Ryan Slater depart for a year-long backpacking trip to Nepal, India, and Sri Lanka. The vision for the Juice Truck is born.

2011

The Juice Truck launches in 2011; it is Canada's first cold-pressed juice bar.

2012

The Juice Truck is featured on the *Food Network*'s popular show Eat St. in 2012.

Eden MacDonald and Colin Medhurst from Feed Life teamed up with the Juice Truck to design and formulate the Juice Cleanse, Vancouver's first home and office juice delivery program.

2013

Suja Juice launches: the first mass-market cold-pressed juice for grocery stores.

2015

Cold-pressed juice has a big year in the press, getting regular attention in the *New York Times*, *Los Angeles Times*, *Economist*, and *Wall Street Journal*.

2016

Cold-pressed juice is named the top wellness trend of the year by the popular health and wellness website *Mindbodygreen*.

THE BASICS

THE KITCHEN

We often say, "My favorite restaurant is my kitchen." You get to be the head chef and create what you love, with the added benefit of knowing exactly what ingredients are going into your meal. The fastest way to turn your kitchen into your favorite restaurant is to make sure you have all the right tools and to lay out your kitchen with a blueprint for success.

The first step to juicing is choosing your produce and ingredients. Scope out a few recipes in advance and stock your pantry accordingly so you're not over-buying and wasting produce or freestyling with whatever is left in the fridge (although sometimes the best juices come from those experiments).

Once you've got your ingredients and you're ready to juice, start by washing your produce. We recommend buying organic and local produce as much as possible to avoid pesticide and herbicide residue. If your fruit and veggies aren't organic, scrub them well with an organic veggie wash (or make your own wash using lemon or apple cider vinegar mixed with water). Peel citrus fruits down to the pith, as the oils in the skin give a bitter flavor. Melons should be peeled as well. Otherwise, you can leave the skin on most produce. Some people prefer to remove the skin from ginger and cucumbers, but as long as they're organic, we like to put these in whole. Remove the pits from plums, peaches, or any other stone fruits. Don't worry about small seeds in lemons, apples, pears, or oranges, as the juicer will spit them out. Then cut the produce to fit the mouth of your juicer.

Now you're ready to juice your washed, peeled, and chopped produce. Juice the stronger flavors first. These are usually the kickers: the ingredients with the highest concentration of flavor, such as ginger or turmeric, or herbs like mint, basil, parsley, or cilantro. Follow those with the leafy greens, and finish with the ingredients with the highest water content. Ingredients with a high liquid content include cucumbers, apples, pears, oranges, carrots, sweet potatoes, pineapples, and melons. Juicing those last helps flush all the other ingredients through and "cleanses the palate" of the juicer to prepare for the next juice.

When you've done all your pressing and your juice is ready to drink, you've got one last step: clean up! Make sure you thoroughly clean your juicer after you use it so you don't clog the screen with pulp, and you don't leave any sticky ickyness to attract fruit flies and other critters.

We want to help you get smart and efficient in the kitchen so it becomes a place of inspiration and creativity, since that is where most of your medicine is made. We're big believers in preventive health, and eating your fruit and veggies is the best way to keep you on that path. Your ability to create nutrient-dense meals for you and your family is a powerful way to ensure long-term health and vitality.

THE FRIDGE

It's important to organize your fridge in a way that makes sense to you so that it becomes a sustainable system. Here are some tips to guarantee an easy and accessible space that keeps produce fresh longer so that you will actually use what you buy. The first step is to place a thermometer in different areas of the fridge to find the warmest and coolest shelves. That will tell you where to put items with a shorter shelf life versus those with longer ones.

THE DOOR

We store condiments that don't need to be kept very cold in the door of the fridge, since it's the warmest area. It's also where we store vitamin powders, coconut water, kelp noodles, ground flax and chia seeds, and soaked and dried nuts and seeds.

TOP SHELF

We keep leftovers, sprouts, and prepackaged items such as hummus, guacamole, salsa, and other dips on the top shelf, so when we are looking for something to eat we look there first. This helps us use up all of the ingredients we buy, and less food gets lost and goes bad. We reserve a container on our top shelves for any leftover fruit and vegetable scraps, which are our go-to items for making juices and smoothies the next day.

TOP MIDDLE SHELF

This is a great place to keep salad toppings, fermented vegetables, and ingredients that are more savory. In other words, flavor and texture components you'd add to complete a meal. For example: nut cheeses, sauerkraut, olives, curry paste, and nut and seed butters.

BOTTOM MIDDLE SHELF

We keep this shelf fully stocked with fresh fruit like berries, avocados, coconut meat, and any other snacks that didn't fit on the top shelf. Organizing the fridge this way gives us a good sense of what we will need before we go grocery shopping. We'll often take a picture of the entire fridge before we leave, so that we know exactly what we need more of.

BOTTOM SHELF

Packaged or loose greens and herbs go here. In the summertime we don't buy packaged greens thanks to the abundance of loose greens available at the farmers' market, which offers a wider variety of ingredients for our juices and smoothies. If possible, place the fresh herbs upright in some water, and to help extend their freshness, snip off the bottom inch and cover them with a plastic bag on top.

BOTTOM DRAWERS

The bottom drawers of the fridge, called crispers, are temperature and humidity controlled. In one drawer, keep your loose leafy greens and green vegetables. We put the heavier vegetables on the bottom and lighter ones on top. In the other drawer, store colorful vegetables. We keep a variety of colors at all times; more colors mean a better variety of nutrients. Also, when doing a pre-shopping check of what you need, you'll be able to see quite quickly how many colors you have left and which colors you need to pick up.

THE PANTRY

Clear glass jars are the key to creating a well-organized pantry space. Using glass jars is an easy way to keep track of how much you have left of an ingredient. If you're new to stocking your pantry full of grains, legumes, and spices, you may want to buy a label maker for quick and accurate identification of your ingredients. We make sure to have a good mix of dried and canned beans and quick- and slow-cooking grains. Having food that can be prepared in minutes reduces the urge to eat out when we've forgotten to plan a meal ahead.

THE SPICE CABINET

Our spice cabinet has a wide variety of spices and salts. We like to think of the spice collection as a palette of flavors when crafting a meal. We keep the cabinet stocked with our regular choices and occasionally buy a few exotic spices and salts to inspire new creativity—the ones that we like, we continue to stock. This expands what we can do with our base ingredients such as greens, grains, and legumes. Spices are best stored in small clear glass jars and only filled halfway, because spices that are opened a lot tend to go stale quite fast. When we buy large bags of dried herbs, we fill the smaller jars whenever they need a top-up and otherwise keep the bags sealed in a cool, dark place. But even stored away, dried herbs and spices have a shelf life; they should be rotated every six months, so try not to buy huge bags that you won't use up. You can also opt for whole spices instead of ground and then grind them yourself (an inexpensive coffee grinder will do the trick). Of all the options, this gives the best and freshest flavor.

THE
PANTRY

- **Dried Herbs and Spices:** thyme, rosemary, sage, oregano, marjoram, basil, chili and chipotle powder, turmeric, garam masala, true cinnamon, mustard seed, coriander, cumin, cardamom, star anise, nutmeg, fennel, pepper, Himalayan salt, raw vanilla powder.
- **Vinegars:** apple cider vinegar, rice wine vinegar, red wine vinegar.
- **Oil:** toasted sesame, coconut, avocado, grapeseed.
- **Grains:** short- and long-grain brown rice, quinoa, brown basmati rice, wild rice, whole seed/grain crackers, brown rice noodles, brown rice cakes.
- **Legumes:** a plethora of lentils and beans. Try them all for their unique flavor profile and nutritional abundance.
- **Other:** ribboned coconut, gluten-free flour, arrowroot powder, baking powder, baking soda, nori sheets (for sushi), kombu, sea vegetable flakes, sun-dried tomatoes, medicinal mushrooms.

THE FRIDGE

- **Condiments:** coconut aminos sauce, miso paste, Dijon mustard, tamarind paste, Thai curry paste, hot sauce.
- **Sweeteners:** coconut nectar, coconut sugar, dates, and date paste.

- **Nuts and seeds:** chia seeds, hemp seeds, Brazil nuts, almonds, walnuts, sunflower seeds, pumpkin seeds, flaxseeds, sesame seeds, tahini, almond butter.
- **Other:** coconut meat, coconut or almond yogurt, tofu, tempeh, kelp noodles, hummus, fermented vegetables, pickles.
- **Medicinal foods:** probiotics, whole-food supplements, liquid blue-green algae, kefir water, kombucha.
- **Produce:** local, seasonal organic fruit and vegetables (make sure to get a variety of colors), sprouts, fresh herbs, ingredients for juice and smoothies.

STARTER SMOOTHIE INGREDIENTS

- **Pantry items:** lucuma, mesquite, maca, cacao, ashwagandha, shilajit, true cinnamon, spirulina, chlorella, aloe vera juice, wheatgrass powder, coconut butter, biofermented brown rice protein, goji berries, other dried berries.
- **Fridge items:** hemp seeds, chia seeds, hemp oil, celery, cucumber, fennel, green apple, banana, orange, berries, greens (kale, Swiss chard, mustard greens, and others), parsley, cilantro, lemon, lime, ginger.

STARTER JUICING INGREDIENTS

- Celery, cucumber, any type of sprout, cabbage, carrot, beet, ginger, fennel, green apple, collard greens, kale, romaine, dandelion greens, wheatgrass, lemon, lime, mint, parsley, cilantro.

THE TOOLS

When embarking on a new practice, having the right tools can be the make or break. They can make your life easier, make goals more attainable, and be the key to making the process enjoyable (and sustainable). We often face two main challenges when starting a new practice:

1. Finding out what tools we *truly* need (read: not making unnecessary purchases).
2. Finding the right tool for us among the array of brands and range of quality goods available.

To help you meet these challenges, we offer you our insight, gained through much trial and error, to get you well equipped so you can make the right choices for your budget, lifestyle, and juicing goals. Your toolbox (and your ingredient list) will expand appropriately as you test and refine different methods, but the information in this chapter offers a foolproof foundation to make this new practice a mainstay.

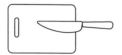

PREPPING FOOD

- Cutting boards
- Knives (serrated knife, 8- to 10-inch chef's knife, paring knife, and sharpening tool)
- Blender (see next page)
- Food processor
- Zester/microplane
- Grater
- Citrus reamer
- Colander
- Sieve
- Can opener

STORAGE

- Glass containers with lids that seal tightly, such as mason jars

COOKING

- Steamer (bamboo or stainless steel)
- Nonstick pans (skillet, pot, saucepan) with lids (remember not to use metal utensils on these to avoid scratching the surfaces). We recommend GreenPan, Woll, or any other nonstick, non-toxic, PTFE-free cookware.
- Cast iron pots and pans are also a good option. Don't forget to season the cast iron for optimal results.

MEASURING

- Measuring spoons
- Measuring cups
- 4-cup glass measuring cup

MIXING/SERVING

- Mixing bowls (small, medium, large)
- Spoons (wooden and slotted)
- Soup ladle
- Flipper
- Rubber spatula
- Double-ended stainless-steel spatula for cleaning out small spaces
- Whisk
- Microplane
- Stainless-steel bowls or glass bowl
- Glass containers with tightly sealing lids, such as mason jars

BAKING

- Baking pan
- Baking sheets
- Casserole pot with lid
- 3-quart rectangular glass baking dish and an 8-inch square dish
- Muffin tin
- Pot holders

BLENDING

A blender is an essential part of your arsenal of kitchen tools for making healthy fast food—from nutritious smoothies to creamy sauces and dips. Here are the main considerations for choosing your first blender.

WHAT IS YOUR BUDGET?

As with most products, you get what you pay for. There is a considerable range of prices: cheaper models will save you money in the short term, but with daily use, an inexpensive blender will lose its power fairly quickly. The more expensive blenders last a long time and are built to pulverize even the toughest ingredients. That said, there are budget-friendly options that have enough power to get the job done.

WHAT ARE YOU USING THE BLENDER FOR?

Most blenders are great with vegetable and fruit smoothies, but if you are planning to make nut milk, nut flour, or nut cheese, you need a blender with enough power to amply pulverize ingredients so you end up with a smooth finished product.

HOW MUCH COUNTER SPACE DO YOU HAVE?

The amount of space available in your kitchen is another consideration, as the powerful machines tend to take up more counter space or cupboard space. Still, we've seen large Vitamix bases proudly stored on the counter, even in the smallest apartment kitchens.

With these considerations in mind, here are two recommendations:

Vitamix: This brand is the gold standard in durability, power, and its ability to puree almost any ingredients into a smooth, creamy texture. We've had the 5200 series for over seven years and use it multiple times a day at home and at all of our nutrition classes. It is a workhorse that just won't quit. All of these machines come with a seven-year warranty, which indicates high quality. However, these machines are not cheap. The company offers certified reconditioned machines if you want quality but don't have $550 or more to spend on a blender.

NutriBullet: This brand is perfect for the budget shopper or someone who doesn't want a huge machine in their small kitchen. We own this machine as well—it's the perfect travel blender. It works best for personal-sized smoothies or sauces and has enough power to blend a nice smoothie and take it to go in the same container (easy cleanup). You can get a NutriBullet for $100.

BLENDING TIPS

- **Drink your smoothie soon after you blend it.** Blended ingredients are exposed to a significant amount of friction, air, and heat, which speeds up oxidation and begins the degradation of nutrients. You can prolong the life of a smoothie by keeping it in an airtight container as full to the top as possible, but the taste and texture may change the longer the smoothie sits.

- **Use cold water instead of ice.** A lot of green smoothie enthusiasts love a cold smoothie, especially on hot days. However, a cold smoothie will slow down your digestive process and may even cause indigestion.

- **Chew your smoothie!** When beginners first try a green smoothie, they often plug their nose and gulp it down. Your digestion begins in your mouth when your food mixes with your saliva, so sip your smoothie slowly and chew it as you would a bite of food to aid complete digestion.

- **Blend in stages.** This step is a must if you are making smoothies with leafy greens and you aren't using a high-powered blender. There is nothing worse than pulling a chunk of kale out of your mouth because it wasn't blended properly. Start with the greens and the liquid, blend until pureed, and then add the remainder of the ingredients.

- **Chop your ingredients.** This helps your blender puree your smoothie faster and puts less stress on the motor. If you have a high-powered blender you don't have to be too picky, but this step will help the less expensive blenders last longer.

- **Add water until the blade is covered first if you are using an upright, low-powered blender.** This prevents ingredients from getting stuck under the blade, which puts extra stress on the motor.

JUICING

A nutrient-rich, enzyme-packed juice starts with the right equipment and some delicious, fresh produce. As with choosing a blender, there are a few things to consider before buying your first juicer to make sure it fits your lifestyle. Since there is a very wide price range to choose from, we recommend choosing a machine within your budget. It may seem obvious, but making a budget-aligned buying decision will make you feel even better about your new juicer and increase the likelihood that juicing becomes part of your long-term routine. And again, consider your space. Make sure you have somewhere to store your juicer that is easy to access, either on your countertop or on an easy-to-reach shelf. If the machine is out of sight, you'll take it out as many times as that dusty casserole dish you were given when you first moved out of your parents' house. And lastly, get clear on what *kind* of juicer you want. An overall rule about juice is that the more air, heat, and friction your juice is exposed to, the faster the enzymes and nutrients break down.

Consumer-grade juicers generally fall into four main categories.

CENTRIFUGAL JUICERS

Centrifugal juicers are the most common juicers found in the market and are generally the most affordable. Fruit and vegetables are pushed down a chute where a fast-spinning blade shreds the ingredients, separating the liquids from the solids (the pulp). The spinning motion of the blade pushes the juice through a mesh basket, and the pulp, in most models, is separated into a separate container.

TO NOTE

These juicers work well with most fruit and vegetables, but they don't extract much juice from leafy greens, grasses, or sprouts. Juice from a centrifugal juicer should be drunk shortly after it's made, because the juice is exposed to a lot of oxygen and friction during extraction. This increases the speed of nutrient breakdown, and decreases the useful life of the juice. All juice should be drunk as soon as possible, but that is especially true for juice made from a centrifugal juicer.

THE PROS
Centrifugal juicers are usually the easiest to use and least expensive.

THE CONS
The heat produced by the fast-turning blade causes oxidation, so the juice has a short shelf life and needs to be drunk soon. Centrifugal juicers are also not the best for leafy greens, and the pulp usually comes out quite wet, meaning there is lots of juice left in the pulp that didn't make it into your cup. Centrifugal juicers are on the loud side—the juicer at work sounds like a band saw. It could definitely wake a sleeping child.

MASTICATING JUICERS
Masticating juicers use a single gear that grinds up the fruit and vegetables, which are pushed by an auger through a mesh press, and strains the juice through a stainless-steel screen. They can either be upright or horizontal.

TO NOTE
These versatile juicers excel at juicing all vegetables, fruit, leafy greens and grasses. The slower crushing action exposes the juice to much less oxygen and a little less heat, producing a more nutrient-dense juice that can be saved for up to forty-eight hours. Masticating juicers are also less messy.

THE PROS
Masticating juicers extract more juice then their centrifugal counterparts. As they are "slow juicers," there is less heat and oxidation, meaning more nutrients and enzymes remain intact. You can store the juice for up to forty-eight hours.

THE CONS
Masticating juicers are more expensive, selling for up to $400. The juice produced often contains some fiber and pulp but this can be strained out with a sieve as an extra step.

TRITURATING JUICERS

Triturating juicers are twin-geared versions of the masticating juicer and are in the higher price range. They work even more slowly than masticating juicers, creating a more nutrient- and enzyme-rich juice.

TO NOTE

This method of extraction produces a lot of juice, and the resulting pulp is extremely dry. These machines are also fantastic for creating your own nut and seed butters. Cleaning them can take longer, compared to the centrifugal or masticating models, but the difference is mere minutes once you are familiar with the breakdown and setup. Twin-geared juicers are the best for sprouts and grasses.

THE PROS

As the twin-gear process is slow, reducing the oxidation, the juice retains most of its nutrients. The juice lasts up to seventy-two hours, so you can produce larger batches.

THE CONS

It's a slower process compared to the centrifugal juicer, and the cleanup can be messy and time consuming.

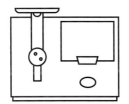

THE NORWALK JUICER

When we started our business, we did a lot of googling, youtubing, tweeting, and field tripping in search of the ultimate juicer. Our research took us to many squeezers, pressers, pulpers, pushers, and a few mysterious "as seen on TV" products. We eventually discovered the wonders of the Norwalk cold-press juicer. This is what we use at the Juice Truck. We consider it the crème de la crème of juicers. It is by far the most expensive of the juicers, but if you are committed to it, the price tag is worth the quality of juice.

Dr. Norman Walker was way ahead of his time. He was mad about raw foods and their health benefits. He invented the Norwalk cold-press juicer in the 1930s. More than eighty-five years later, it still has the same basic design, and it still produces the best, most nutrient-rich juice on the market.

So what is cold pressing? It describes the method of juicing. Most juice bars and many home juicers use a conventional centrifugal juicer, which separates the juice from the pulp with high-speed spinning blades. In contrast to the Norwalk juicer, this process creates a lot of friction, which in turn creates high heat and oxidation, destroying vital nutrients and living enzymes. The Norwalk juicer has two separate juice extraction machines built into it: the pulverizer (this is best said in an Arnold Schwarzenegger accent) and the hydraulic press. A slow spinning blade ("the pulverizer") creates a pulp out of the produce, which is then wrapped in a cotton or linen cloth and placed on a tray in preparation for the hydraulic press. The juice is extracted through the tremendous pressure exerted by the hydraulic press. Maximal amounts of vitamins, trace minerals, live enzymes, phytonutrients, and other vital elements are preserved. All the while, minimal amounts of friction, heat, and oxidation occur. The cold press makes for the most vitamin-packed super juice (superpowers may follow).

TO NOTE

If you want to produce large batches to be drunk over two to three days, the Norwalk is the best. If you're going to do juice cleanses, the Norwalk will produce the juices with the most health benefits. The Norwalk juicer can also create nut butter, nut flours, and vegan "ice cream."

THE PROS

The cold-pressed juicer produces almost no oxidization, resulting in the most nutrient- and enzyme-rich juice possible. Because of the limited heat and oxidization, the juice is shelf stable for seventy-two (refrigerated) hours. It extracts almost twice as much juice as a centrifugal juicer and 50 percent more juice then a masticating juicer, and is fairly quick and easy to clean.

THE CONS

The cold press is the most expensive option, costing up to $2,000. It's also a slower process, taking ten to fifteen minutes to make a batch of juice.

OUR JUICER OF CHOICE

When we founded the Juice Truck in 2011, we chose to juice with Norwalk hydraulic cold-press juicers. There are companies working on launching other cold-press juicers, but currently Norwalk is the only cold-press juicer made for home use. We went with cold pressing for a couple of reasons:

1. To offer juice with the best nutritional value by using the juicer that oxidizes least.
2. To produce juice with a reasonable shelf life to avoid waste.

We were the first juicery in Canada to offer cold-pressed juice to order and we are still one of the only companies in the world to offer it. We believe that our regulars have been such loyal customers over the years because we serve the healthiest, most enzyme- and nutrient-rich juice you could possibly have.

Regardless of which juicer you choose, the most important thing is your commitment to using it. The different features we list above are mere details. While making the best buying choice for your kitchen and your wallet *does* matter, whatever you decide to buy is perfect.

When you spend your hard-earned money on a juicer, you aren't just adding to the appliances in your kitchen; you are opening up a whole new world of consistent access to concentrated nutrition. The beginning of a regular juicing practice is the best part—a time when increased energy, clear skin, and a general shift in overall healthy feeling reigns supreme.

THE LIFESTYLE

DITCH THE TRENDS

It seems like every week there is a new health trend, fad diet, or way to lose weight. Don't eat carbs. Eat carbs. Only eat carbs that are not processed. It's hard to keep up with so many contrasting ideas being broadcast everywhere. What we know is that there's no quick fix for lasting health. Health and well-being come from more than just what you're eating; they're about how you're living. We like to make choices that are easy to live by and easy to sustain. Most of our suggestions for a healthy lifestyle are common sense—they're ideas you're probably already familiar with. But it's these easy-to-follow lifestyle reminders that keep life in balance for us and might prove helpful to you as you begin your own juicing journey.

JUICING SHOULD BE FUN

For something to become part of your routine—a daily ritual, a habit—it needs to be something that you look forward to. Our first step to creating a balanced lifestyle with serious health benefits is to make it *fun*. Make it playful. Include your friends and family and try out different ingredient combinations by sharing recipes. The journey is more fun when you're heading there with a group that you can share the experience with.

BRING IT BACK TO BALANCE

We believe that balanced individuals create a balanced environment and a balanced world. If you're making mindful decisions about the food you're putting into your body, it will create a balanced, healthy body and result in a positive agricultural impact, which, in turn, has a positive effect on the environment.

FOCUS ON HOW YOU *FEEL* VERSUS A RESULT

Set goals to feel a certain way instead of obsessing over numbers on a scale or inches lost. For instance, you might find that working out with your community makes exercise fun. And once it becomes fun, you almost forget that it's a workout . . . almost. The positive group environment and good vibes from the connections and the workout make your heart feel good. And before you know it, you'll feel good about the changes that you'll see and sense in your body. The same can be said about juicing. Get your family, friends, or neighbors involved. When it becomes a community activity, it will soon become routine, and a part of your day you look forward to.

START YOUR DAY WITH INTENTION

State the day's purpose when you wake up. "I choose to be happy." "I'm going to start my day with the best green juice." "I am going to make time for yoga today." Rather than falling into the trap of mindless routine (even if your routine already includes juicing, yoga, etc.), start your day with clear focus and intention. The presence you bring to your activities will have a positive impact on you and those around you. Starting each day with intention has helped us maintain a positive outlook, stay on track with our goals, and handle unplanned surprises.

STAYING GROUNDED IS KEY

Making meditation a daily practice is one way to ground yourself. You don't have to sit cross-legged searching for nirvana; meditation can take many forms. For us, it's usually a quiet walk or hike in nature at least once a week. Being in nature liberates our minds and makes way for creativity. It can be a place for inner reflection and quiet, or a place for discussion and brainstorming with others. Working out is another form of meditation. Even watching the right movie or reading a book can give our minds the break we need to stay grounded and be mindful. Change it up and find what works for you; just like juicing, it's got to be fun. Otherwise, you won't do it.

MOVEMENT

We are made to move. Sitting at desks, lying on the couch, scrolling social media; it's all contrary to what our bodies are built for. Movement boosts circulation, eases tension, stimulates your metabolism, releases endorphins, boosts libido—we've got to keep on moving! You don't need to run for hours on a treadmill or become a gym junkie to get moving. Find what works for you and make it a habit. Just like brushing your teeth, movement should be part of your daily routine.

The more you use your muscles, the more they increase in strength, size, and stamina. It's the best possible domino effect. When you move, your muscles need more oxygen. Your heart works harder to pump blood through your body, making your cardiovascular system stronger and more efficient. That means it gets better at circulating oxygen even when you're relaxing and taking it easy.

Here are some more benefits to movement:

Lymphatic drainage. The lymphatic system is a network of tiny vessels that makes up a big part of our immune system. Unlike the bloodstream, the lymphatic system doesn't have a built-in pump. It relies solely on muscle contraction to move the lymph toward the heart. If you don't move, the system breaks down. Jump on a rebounder or trampoline, use a dry brush, go for a run, pound on your chest like Tarzan (no really, this actually helps) . . . it all helps keep the lymph moving.

Brain health. Exercising is essential to optimal cognitive function. We certainly find that whenever we are active, our mood seems to improve. Exercise releases neurotransmitters such as dopamine, serotonin, and endorphins—all chemicals that provide a feeling of elation or happiness. When you exercise and your heart gets pumping, your blood transports more oxygen throughout your body. This leads to your brain producing new neurons and repairing damaged ones, and promotes overall mental well-being.

Weight loss. Though we're more focused on the fun and feeling side of movement, weight loss is a natural by-product of exercise. If you expend more energy than you take in—burn more calories than you consume—you're going to lose weight.

FOOD

Here's one that many of us are guilty of: overeating. Eating until we're full and then maybe eating just a little bit more. We've come a long way since we ate with the seasons as hunters and gatherers. Sadly, that's not necessarily a good thing. Gone are the days when the everyday person worked the soil, planted the seed, harvested the produce, hunted, foraged, and gathered. Today, we can have fast food delivered to our house without leaving the couch, and everything is accessible at any time in our grocery stores, often packaged and processed.

Being so disconnected from where our food comes from is concerning. Mindless eating takes a toll on the dwindling environment and on our bodies. But we think there is power in the decision to eat mindfully. A few rules we live by:

Eat with awareness. Whenever we prepare our own food, we know exactly what we are putting into our bodies. The experience of touching, smelling, and handling every ingredient in a meal connects you further to the process while priming your body for digestion. If you can get your produce from your backyard garden or a farmers' market and prepare the meal yourself, the experience and connection are very different from buying something in a can or a package that's ready to be microwaved.

Eat slowly. We like to say, "Drink your solids and chew your fluids." Digestion starts in your mouth: the act of chewing breaks down your food, and the digestive enzymes in your saliva take it from there. Chewing slowly is another step to being connected to your food. The opposite—eating quickly—can lead to gas, bloating, and reflux as you swallow more air the quicker you gulp things down. Chewing slowly and savoring your food gives your taste buds extra satisfaction, while sending the message to your brain that you're full, reducing the chance of overeating.

Eat whole foods. We are cautious of any packaged foods that contain more than four ingredients, especially if we don't know how to pronounce the words. The more processed the food (that is, the more ingredients), the harder your body has to work to extract nutrients. Stick to simple whole foods: kale is kale, spinach is spinach, and so on. Plus, processed foods are often packed with toxins that can be harmful in large doses. The less toxins in your diet, the easier it is for your body to run at optimal capacity. Just like overly processed foods, we tend to avoid GMOs (genetically modified organisms). Whenever possible, choose local and organic. Organic foods are free of residual synthetic fertilizers, herbicides, and pesticides. And, in our opinion, they taste much better. When you eat organic, you don't have to eat as much, as nutrient-dense foods fill you up and give you more energy. Also, eating locally brings more awareness to the seasonality of food, and eating with the seasons is what the body naturally craves.

Have fun. Eat what you enjoy! If your diet consists exclusively of restrictions, rules, and counting this and that, odds are that eating will be stressful for you. Ultimately, your body knows what it wants and needs, and when it's had enough. Your body will tell you when you've eaten too much, or had something that doesn't agree with you. Take the time to listen to your body and enjoy your meals. After all, connecting over great food is one of the most enjoyable human experiences. Mix things up with your juice, too. Sometimes the craziest, silliest, strangest combinations are the ones you end up going back to time after time. See how spiciness, or mintiness, or another flavor combination can hit the right spots on your palate!

THE FOUR PILLARS OF A HEALTHY DIET

If you think of your health like your house, you need four walls to make that house stand. Here are our four pillars that lead to balanced health. Follow these suggestions and you won't easily be blown over . . . no matter how big the wolf.

1. PLANT-BASED

Plant foods such as vegetables, grains, legumes, nuts, seeds, and fruit should ideally make up the majority of your daily diet. Our personal ideal amount of plant-based foods consumed is 100 percent. However, changes don't happen overnight. Set a goal and take steps toward a more plant-based diet, and most importantly a diet that works for you. We often find a good first step is to add rather than subtract. Try adding more plants to your current diet and slowly making adjustments toward a more plant-forward diet. A great goal to work toward is a diet that consists of 80 percent plant-based foods and 20 percent other foods of your choice.

2. WHOLE FOOD

Whole foods are unprocessed, unrefined, and as close to nature as you can find them. As soon as you start to process and change a plant from its original form, you start to lose vitamins, minerals, enzymes, and phytonutrients. Processed, fast, and refined foods are designed to appeal to our inherent preference for sweet, salt, and fat to create something that tastes better than the other foods on the market. These three components of eating are all essential for survival—calories, minerals, and fat, but as people eat more and more processed foods, their taste palates shift from enjoying natural flavors that are only subtly sweet and salty to requiring more to feel satiated.

3. NUTRIENT DENSE

Colorful, whole plant foods contain over ten thousand phytochemicals. Many of these phytochemicals have been shown to protect against cancer and other disease. By transitioning from a calorie-dense diet to a nutrient-dense diet, you provide your body with a full spectrum of nutrients to aid in the protection, repair, detoxification, and proper functioning of your body.

Foods that are in their whole-food form, are rich with color, are in season, have not traveled far from where they were picked, and have ripened naturally have the most vitamins, minerals, enzymes, and phytonutrients.

If you were to take all the vitamins, minerals, enzymes, phytonutrients, protein, fat, and carbohydrates and average them out over the calories per serving size of a single ingredient, leafy greens are the food with the highest nutrient density.

4. INCLUDES HEALTHY FATS

Fat is essential for health. Omega-6 and omega-3 fatty acids are fats that we must ingest from our diet. Unfortunately, most people are deficient in omega-3 fats and eat too many omega-6 fats. Omega-3 is critical for fighting inflammation, the formation of our cells, the health of our skin, emotional well-being, a healthy heart, and more. Seeds like chia, flaxseed, and hemp are high in omega-3s, as are leafy greens, beans, cabbage, and winter squash. Avocado, soybeans, walnuts, Brazil nuts, and sesame seeds are all great sources of omega-6. If you're pressed for squeezing in enough omega-rich foods, we recommend taking an algae-based DHA supplement.

ORGANICS 101

We choose organic because it's more nutrient dense and better for the environment. Organic plants are more nutrient dense because they have to develop a stronger immune system. When a plant is covered in pesticides and herbicides it doesn't defend itself against fungus, bacteria, and pests, so it is not as rich in protective phytonutrients. When we eat an organic plant, rich with phytonutrients developed to protect it, our bodies use the nutrients to protect and strengthen themselves. Organically grown plants may also be more nutrient dense and higher in protein. Heavily fertilized conventional or non-organic plants grow fast but are undernourished and are lower in nutrients.

Want to start buying more organic produce but don't know how to keep it within your budget? Check out the Environmental Working Group (www.ewg.org)—they have created a great resource. Their "Dirty Dozen" and "Clean Fifteen" lists tell you which non-organic foods have the most and least pesticide use to help you prioritize which produce to buy organic. There is also a helpful smartphone app that you can consult while shopping. Shopping at your farmers' market is another great way of reducing your shopping bill—buy direct from the farm to your plate. Buy large quantities of seasonal produce at a discounted rate and then turn them into pickles, chutneys, or broth to preserve them, or freeze them into serving sizes so you can pull one out during times of the year when fresh produce is harder to find.

IF YOU THINK OF YOUR HEALTH LIKE A HOUSE, YOU NEED FOUR WALLS TO MAKE THAT HOUSE STAND.

THE
BASE.

Cucumber, celery, pear,
kale, lemon, & ginger

Concombre, céleri, poire,
chou, citron, & gingembre

THE
JUICE
TRUCK

500 mL

WHAT IS PLANT-BASED?

We use the term *plant-based* instead of *vegan*, although that is essentially how our menu is made up at the Juice Truck. Plant-based implies that the food is predominantly plants while leaving room for other foods in smaller condiment-sized amounts. We like how using the term *plant-based* allows people to make nutrient-dense choices without having to feel guilty when they want to indulge in other foods. Guilt is not a sustainable way to create change. As David Wolfe, a leader in the raw superfood movement, says, "The best strategy we've got is to just add the good stuff! Eventually it's going to crowd out the bad stuff."

We believe the ideal diet for our bodies is primarily a plant-based diet. We also believe that the ideal diet for healing our planet is plant-based. They both just happen to be the same, and that makes us even more passionate about talking to people about the many health benefits.

Most people intuitively know that healthy eating equals eating whole, unprocessed foods. Only recently has the conventional scientific community begun to embrace that diet has a huge impact on our health. Now research is overwhelmingly pointing to the fact that a diet including fresh, whole foods is directly related to the prevention of disease. If a plant-based diet interests you, try it out for yourself and see how amazing you can feel in just a few short weeks—you will likely notice in the first few days that you are lighter and more energetic.

OUR TOP REASONS TO EAT MORE PLANTS

Growing up, we all had ideas about what it meant to be vegetarian. Smells of patchouli and frankincense come to mind. Tofu everything. Supplements galore. Tie-dyed dresses. But jumping forward to the modern day, we see that vegetarian eating has come a long way. Most restaurants embrace plant-based options, and the community has grown immensely. As our world continues to change, the need to eat more plant-based has become more significant. Our food choices greatly affect our bodies and our environment.

There are lots of different reasons to go plant-based. Weight loss, increased energy, environmental concerns, reduced risk of heart disease, compassion for animals . . . the list goes on and on. By eating nothing but plants you can live a healthier, more sustainable life. You'd be surprised how quickly you reach a healthy body weight, your skin will clear up and glow, your mental state will sharpen, and your sleep will improve. As simple as it sounds, eating plants, close to their natural state, can transform your body, mind, and spirit.

Health begins with what we put on our plates. But that's just the starting point. True wellness goes beyond us to the collective sustainability and vitality of all living things. So here's how we break it down: our top reasons to go plant-based to live a healthier and more responsible life.

1. SAVE THE PLANET

We all share the responsibility to protect the earth and the billions of people and animals that we share it with. Eating a plant-based diet is the biggest way to make a positive impact on your personal health and the health of our environment. Global emissions from agriculture (livestock and crops) is the largest contributor to greenhouse gas emissions, more than the exhaust of all transportation modes combined. Eighteen percent of global emissions come directly from livestock. This stat doesn't adequately account for CO_2 produced by the respiration of tens of billions of farm animals. It's estimated that livestock could be responsible for up to 51 percent of global emissions. Adopting a plant-based diet could cut your carbon footprint by 50 percent.

Animal agriculture is also a leading cause of wildlife habitat loss, water shortage, deforestation, and species extinction. About 2,500 gallons of water are needed to produce just one pound of beef in North America. In the US, agriculture is responsible for almost 90 percent of water use. In fact, the meat and dairy industry uses one third of the entire planet's fresh water, and livestock covers 45 percent of the earth's total land. In terms of land use, one and a half acres of land can produce 37,000 pounds of plant food compared to only 375 pounds of meat. That means a meat eater needs eighteen times as much land necessary to feed someone eating plant-based.

The oceans aren't bearing well either. They're being depleted of fish at an alarming rate. Many studies say that our oceans may be fishless by 2048. The current food system, based on meat and dairy production, works against solving world hunger, as the majority of crops grown globally go toward feeding livestock, not feeding people.

Equally important, animals raised for food, just like us, are sentient, intellectual, emotional beings, who feel joy as well as suffering. Eating a plant-based diet helps us live a compassionate life that is mindful of our relationship with the environment and the animals that coexist with us. Coming full circle, living a healthy lifestyle is more than food choices; it's also about our consciousness—our awareness of how our choices affect the planet and all those we share it with.

2. HELP PREVENT SPECIES EXTINCTION

Animal agriculture is the leading cause of species extinction, ocean dead zones, water pollution, and habitat destruction. It is responsible for over 91 percent of the destruction of the Amazon rainforest. By the time you finish reading this sentence, 1 to 2 acres of rainforest will have been cleared. To date, 136 million acres of rainforest have been cleared for animal agriculture. With that, more than 130 plant, animal, and insect species are lost every day due to rainforest destruction.

In addition to the immense habitat destruction caused by clearing forests and altering the land to grow feed crops and graze animals, predator species are frequently targeted, hunted, and killed because they are perceived as threats to livestock profits. Top it all off with the rampant use of pesticides, herbicides, and chemical fertilizers in the production of feed crops. These chemicals often interfere with the reproductive systems of animals, and they poison waterways that are habitats and water sources for animals.

Meanwhile, in the oceans, the overexploitation of fish and ocean animals through commercial fishing is contributing to a worldwide depletion of species and resources. Three quarters of the world's fisheries are either extremely exploited or completely depleted. Each year, 90 to 100 million tons of fish and marine animals (which is as many as 2.7 trillion animals) are pulled from our oceans. For every pound of fish caught, up to 5 pounds of unintended marine species are caught and thrown out as by-kill. It's estimated that as many as 650,000 whales, dolphins, and seals are killed every year by the fishing industry, which sadly doesn't even come close to the 40 to 50 million sharks that have been killed in fishing lines and nets. We need to start protecting the biodiversity that is essential to maintain the healthy ecology of our planet before it's too late.

3. REDUCE INFLAMMATION IN YOUR BODY

If meat, dairy, and processed foods are a regular part of your diet, there's a good chance your body has high levels of inflammation. Short-term inflammation is normal and necessary, especially after a sports injury or an extra-hard workout. However, long-lasting inflammation that lingers for months or years is not safe or healthy. Chronic inflammation has been linked to atherosclerosis, heart attacks, strokes, diabetes, and autoimmune diseases, among other conditions.

Plant-based diets have just the opposite effect. A plant-based diet is high in fiber, antioxidants, and other phytonutrients leading to natural anti-inflammatory benefits. Fruits, vegetables, nuts, and seeds have far fewer inflammatory catalysts like saturated fat and endotoxins (toxins released from bacteria, most commonly found in animal products). Lowering inflammation in your body makes maintaining an active, healthy lifestyle that much easier.

4. ENJOY THE BENEFITS OF NUT MILK

Most of the world can't digest dairy. According to the Physicians Committee for Responsible Medicine, more than 65 percent of the world's population is genetically unable to digest dairy products. More dairy does not equal stronger bones; vitamin D is more protective than calcium for bone density. And if you are unable to digest lactose and consume dairy, you'll have an inflammatory reaction. Also, dairy contains more than just milk! Dairy can contain hormones, growth factors, antibiotics, and pus, all of which can hurt your health.

Nut milk is a clean, nutrient-dense alternative to dairy. It can be low in fat, but high in energy, proteins, healthy fatty acids, and fiber. It contains minerals like calcium, iron, magnesium, phosphorus, potassium, and zinc. Each nut offers a variety of benefits and flavors. They're quick, fun, and easy to make, and you'll be amazed with how good nut milk tastes!

On top of this, animal products are acid forming, which means they promote calcium loss from your bones. Countries that consume the most cow's milk and dairy by-products have the highest bone fracture rates. In contrast, in countries where 90 percent of dietary protein is derived from plant sources, one fifth of the bone fractures were reported. Contrary to all the advertising, milk doesn't do a body good.

5. LOWER YOUR BLOOD CHOLESTEROL LEVELS

High blood cholesterol is a major risk factor for heart disease and strokes, two of the leading causes of death in North America. Saturated fat, which is mainly found in meat, poultry, cheese, and other animal products, is a main contributor to blood cholesterol levels. Cholesterol in our food plays a role as well. Studies consistently show blood cholesterol levels drop by up to 35 percent when people go plant-based.

Plant-based diets reduce blood cholesterol because a plant-based, whole-food diet is generally very low in saturated fat and cholesterol. Plant-based diets are also very high in fiber, which helps further reduce blood cholesterol levels.

6. HAVE A HAPPY GUT—WHICH EQUALS A HAPPY BODY

The trillions of microorganisms living in our bodies are collectively called the microbiome. They are major players in helping us digest our food, plus they produce important nutrients, help train our immune systems, turn genes on and off, keep our gut tissue healthy, and protect us from diseases. If that's not enough, they have also been shown to play a role in obesity, diabetes, atherosclerosis, autoimmune disease, inflammatory bowel disease, and liver disease.

A plant-based diet helps maintain and boost a healthy intestinal microbiome. Fiber in plant foods promotes the growth of healthy bacteria in our guts. In contrast, diets low in fiber (such as those high in dairy, eggs, and meat) can promote the growth of disease-promoting bacteria. When we consume choline or carnitine (found in meat, poultry, seafood, eggs, and dairy), our gut bacteria create a substance that is converted by our liver to a toxic product called TMAO. TMAO harbors the growth of cholesterol plaques in our blood vessels, which increases the risk of heart attack and stroke.

A plant-based meal creates little to no TMAO in comparison to a meal based on meat and dairy, as they interact with a totally different gut microbiome. Interestingly, it takes only a few days for our populations of gut bacteria to change. You'll notice the benefits of a plant-based diet almost immediately.

7. CHANGE THE WAY YOUR GENES WORK

Studies have established that lifestyle and environmental factors can turn genes on and off. For example, when we eat whole plant foods, the antioxidants and nutrients from the plants can change gene expression to optimize how our cells repair damaged DNA. Research has shown that a plant-based lifestyle can lengthen our telomeres (the caps at the ends of our chromosomes that help keep our DNA stable). This can cause our cells and tissues to age more slowly, as shortened telomeres are linked with aging and earlier death.

8. REDUCE YOUR ODDS OF GETTING TYPE 2 DIABETES

It's estimated that almost 40 percent of Americans have prediabetes. Protein derived from animal products (most specifically red meat and processed meat), increases the risk of type 2 diabetes. Studies show that omnivores have double the rate of diabetes compared to vegans. Over a seventeen-year study, people who ate meat once a week or more were 74 percent more likely to develop diabetes than vegetarians! Further research shows that increasing red meat consumption by more than just half a serving per day equates to a 48 percent increased risk in diabetes over four years.

So why does eating meat cause type 2 diabetes? Animal fat, animal-source iron, and nitrate preservatives in meat damage pancreatic cells, worsen inflammation, cause weight gain, and impair how our insulin functions. Not eating animal products and eating a diet based in whole plant foods will dramatically lessen your chances of getting type 2 diabetes. Regularly eating whole grains, which are highly protective against type 2 diabetes, will further the cause. If you are already diabetic, eating a plant-based diet can improve and even reverse type 2 diabetes.

9. PROTEIN! GET THE RIGHT AMOUNT OF IT!

Most people in North America get more than one and a half times the recommended amount of daily protein, and most of it from animal sources. Contrary to popular belief, excess protein does not make you stronger, nor does it make you leaner. Your body stores excess protein as fat or turns it into waste. Animal protein can be a major contributor to weight gain, heart disease, diabetes, and inflammation.

In contrast, the protein from whole plant-based foods helps protect us from many chronic diseases. Think of Popeye. He was ahead of his time, getting protein to support his active lifestyle through his ideal superfood: spinach! As long as your daily calorie needs are met and you're eating a plant-based diet, you will get plenty of protein. Gorillas, giraffes, rhinos, and elephants are all strong animals on a 100 percent vegetarian diet.

10. FEED THE WORLD

On this earth, people are dying of starvation every minute, yet studies show that we are currently growing enough food to comfortably feed 10 billion people. The US alone could feed more than 800 million people with the grain that is used to feed livestock. There really is no reason for anyone to go hungry. Starvation has more to do with allocation and distribution of food than scarcity.

11. PREVENT (AND REVERSE) CHRONIC DISEASE

North America is obsessed with weight loss. We're in the midst of an obesity epidemic in North America, and we're clinically the sickest region of the world. Overeating has evolved through processed and fast foods, and this fast-food lifestyle is quite literally killing us. Heart disease is the leading cause of death in the US and the second leading cause, behind cancer, in Canada. One out of every four Americans dies of heart disease. Seventy percent of Americans and 40 percent of Canadians are obese or overweight, and it's predicted that within the next fifteen years 50 percent of adult Americans and nearly 25 percent of Canadians will be diabetic or pre-diabetic. We struggle with unsustainable crash diets and weight-loss plans. We spend more on weight loss than any other continent yet we have more cases of obesity.

Our food choices can lead to disease and death, or to health and longevity. A healthy diet can be the best preventative health care available. A plant-based diet has been proven to prevent and even reverse disease. Studies have shown that a plant-based dietary approach leads to larger short-term and long-term improvements in dietary inflammatory and macronutrient intake compared with diets that contain meat. It's time for us to get informed and make empowered decisions regarding our health and the food that we eat.

12. MAKE YOUR SKIN GLOW

The easiest (and cheapest) way to have healthy, glowing skin is to eat a clean, healthy diet, while avoiding processed foods, meat, and dairy. Your hair, your eyes, your skin, and your nails will all gleam with a healthy glow from a plant-based diet. The detoxifying effect of eating plants, the boosted elimination benefits, plus the ease with which plants are digested all lead to less internal toxins that cause acne and more nutrients to make our hair shine and our skin glow. Fruit and vegetables are naturally dense with beautifying substances like vitamin C, which boosts collagen and smooths wrinkles; lycopene, which helps protect skin from the sun; and antioxidants like lutein and beta-carotene, which help soften the skin and keep it looking supple.

13. GET LOTS OF CALCIUM

You get all the calcium you need on a plant-based diet. Calcium is an essential mineral for helping our body remodel our bones and keep them strong. North Americans have a high incidence of osteoporosis (weakening of the bones). This can be caused by eating large amounts of animal protein from meat, eggs, and dairy, which actually leaches calcium from the bones.

As long as you eat enough calories per day and limit your sodium intake, you are sure to get enough calcium on a plant-based diet by including these great foods: sesame seeds, nuts, legumes, whole grains, broccoli, celery, and green, leafy vegetables such as Swiss chard, romaine lettuce, kale, and watercress.

(BONUS) LOSE WEIGHT

Plants are generally low in calories and high in nutrients. Calorie for calorie, plants give your body the biggest nutritional bang for your buck. This nutrient density results in you needing less food to feel fuller. Also, plants are high in fiber and keep

you regular, which helps you stay slim. As plants, especially in their raw form, are nutrient packed, your body has less work to do in digesting food. Since plant foods require so little digestion, the nutrients are quickly absorbed resulting in almost instant and long-lasting energy. This abundant energy will help you with your physical exercise and staying in shape.

In addition to dropping a few pounds, you'll also probably see a drop in your cholesterol. Though your genes have an influence on your cholesterol level, a plant-based diet can have an effect, because only foods derived from animals contain cholesterol.

There's no need to put labels on it—vegan, plant-based, omnivore, or flexitarian— no matter what you call it, eating more plants is one of the most profound and life-altering choices you can make. We feel it's one of the most effective ways to live a conscious and compassionate life. A plant-based diet will help prevent and

reverse disease, greatly reduce your carbon footprint, and preserve our world for many generations to come. Whether you are a doctor, a naturopath, someone who follows the paleo diet, a vegan, an omnivore, or the person who orders a side of bacon with everything, we can all agree that eating whole, plant-based foods means more nutrients, vitamins, minerals, antioxidants, fiber, and healthy fats. We all need these things for optimal health. Go for the greens, spread the word, and do your part to change the world, one bite at a time! Or better yet, get a running start by trying out the juice and smoothie recipes in this book.

GO FOR THE GREENS. SPREAD THE WORD. ONE BITE AT A TIME.

THE CLEANSE

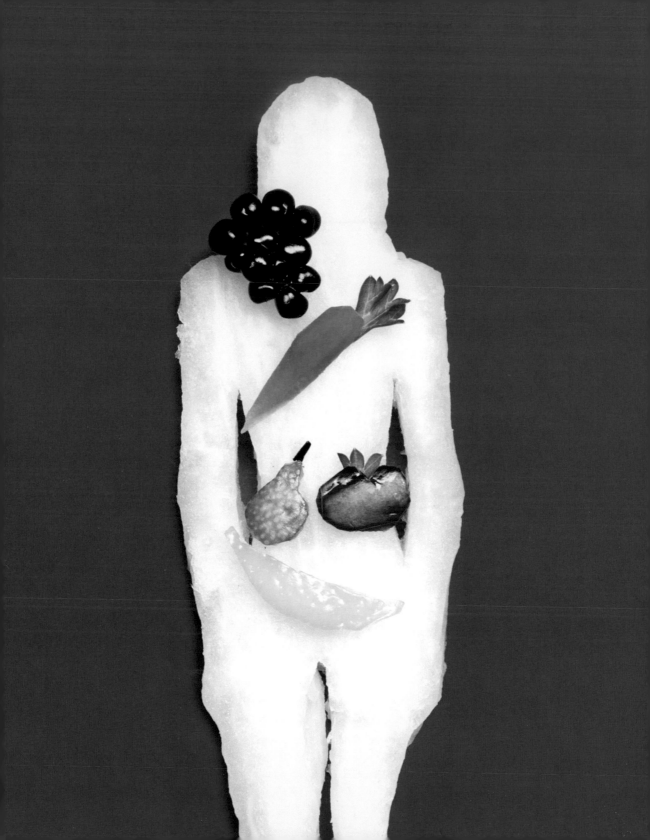

THE BENEFITS

We believe detoxification is essential to a healthy body, mind, and spirit. Usually, your body will show signs of distress well before any illness sets in: headaches, constipation, fatigue, body odor, bad breath, acne or skin problems, weight issues, gas, bloating, allergies—the list goes on. What we sometimes perceive as "everyday issues" can be caused by a buildup of toxins within the body. So when they start showing up, we take it as a hint that it's time for a detox.

Detoxification or cleansing practices have been recorded throughout history, even appearing in religious texts. The practice of cleansing has roots within many of our traditional healing systems. Cleansing has long been seen as a way to reset your body's natural detoxification systems and maintain an internal environment that is resilient to disease. Health and wellness author Annemarie Colbin wrote, "Entire religions have evolved from one man's fast, empires toppled, wars halted. For examples we need look no further than Jesus, Muhammad, the Buddha, Gandhi." Jesus fasted for forty days and nights. Islam has Ramadan. Judaism has Yom Kippur. The early great philosophers, thinkers, and healers used fasting and detoxing for health and as healing therapy. Hippocrates, Plato, Socrates, Aristotle, and Galen all promoted the benefits of fasting and detoxifying the body.

Yes, our bodies do naturally eliminate toxins, specifically through the bladder, bowel, liver, kidneys, lungs, and skin. But these organs can become overworked from stress, processed and fast foods, toxic and polluted environments, and overly acidic diets. With all of these stimulants, the body can accumulate more toxins than its elimination channels can handle.

Cleansing is a great way to give your body a vacation from unhealthy food choices, dehydration, and excess. When was the last time your digestive system got a vacation? Probably when you got the flu and didn't feel like eating for a few days.

The reality is that nobody is perfect. We'd all like to think that our diet is pretty good and we take care of ourselves. And it's hard to know what to do with all the information about health that we are inundated with. Should we eat raw all the time? Eat paleo, macrobiotic, drink wheatgrass shots three times a day, take coconut oil by the spoonful, eat hemp or whey protein? Let's face it: everyone has their own opinion on what a healthy diet should be, but we do know some things for certain. We know a healthy diet includes lots of colorful fruit and vegetables—and yet most people do not consume enough of these! The principle behind cleansing is to infuse your body with nutrient-dense calories so you can reconnect with the food you should be eating all the time.

Even if you have the cleanest diet and you break a sweat every day, you are still exposed to toxins. Research shows that the average person is exposed to thousands of toxins and environmental pollutants daily.

Here are just some sources of toxicity:

- Prescription drugs
- Cleaning products
- Dry-cleaning chemicals
- Air fresheners
- Preservatives and additives in foods
- Alcohol
- Smoking
- Recreational drugs
- Refined and processed foods

So, while our bodies are built to eliminate toxins and waste, they need a tune-up every now and again to function at their optimal performance. This is where the principle of seasonal cleansing comes in. Eating a nutrient-dense, plant-based diet will infuse your body with life-giving nutrients and help you to refresh, renew, and rebalance your body for your new healthy eating path, whatever form it takes!

Cleansing supports all your body's detoxification systems. It's important that the body is cleansed in the proper order. If you cleanse the liver without cleansing the intestines first, the toxins may get stuck in the intestines, which could lead to impaired digestion and absorption of nutrients. Juicing, smoothies, and nutrient-dense, plant-based food naturally give you specific nutrients to gently detoxify (and we promise, the juices taste great too!).

Your detoxification organs and pathways:

Liver: The liver is the main detoxification organ. It works around the clock to detoxify the body, and we rely on it to do over five hundred different jobs. When we are exposed to too many toxins, the liver can become overwhelmed. The toxins lodge in cells and tissues or get stored in fat cells. The body is constantly trying to find a balance (homeostasis) by trying to clean out these toxins through the skin, lungs, and kidneys. Side effects of our bodies trying to deal with these toxins can be pimples, rashes, cold and flus, headaches, aches and pains, and fatigue.

Kidneys: The kidneys filter metabolic waste out of the blood and regulate the pH of the body. They excrete toxins by creating urine out of blood plasma.

Colon: The colon is responsible for absorbing nutrients and carrying waste out of the body.

Lungs: Without oxygen, our body cannot create energy from the food we eat. Toxins are either trapped in the mucous lining of our lungs and coughed up, or breathed out.

Lymph: Lymph surrounds our cells and carries nourishment to the body and clears out waste. Unlike the blood, which relies on the heart to pump it through the body, the lymphatic system requires gravity and movement (exercise) to drive circulation.

Skin: Skin is the largest elimination organ! Exercise to get your heart beating and your skin sweating. Sweat helps cleanse toxins from your body. Another option is dry brushing, which is one of the best ways to help your skin detoxify.

What are some of the possible benefits of cleansing?

- Increased stamina and mental clarity
- Glowing skin
- Shiny hair and strong nails
- Fewer colds and viruses
- Improved liver function and digestion
- Reduction in hay fever and allergies
- Fewer cravings for sugar and refined foods
- Better sleep
- Increased energy
- Fewer aches and pains

Simply put, detoxification is the process of helping the body purge toxins that have accumulated in many different types of cells. Detoxifying helps your organs work more effectively and puts less stress on your body when you indulge in a bit too much junk food.

JUICE AND SMOOTHIE CLEANSING

We believe creating nutrient-dense smoothies and juices is the most convenient way to get a lot of nutrients into an easy-to-drink, delicious glass of nutritive wellness. We use the cleansing recipes provided in this book to support our bodies' own detoxification systems. To do the same, invest some time in creating, preparing, and organizing some of your blended meals. You'll save time, and you won't be chained to the kitchen for the duration of your cleanse. The main benefits of juicing are that you'll be able to consume a large amount of the necessary vitamins, minerals, amino acids, and phytochemicals in a single sitting. Blending and juicing also predigest the meal, so your body can focus on absorption, healing, and detoxification.

THE CLEANSE STEPS

Cleansing is far more enjoyable and efficient if you remove certain foods from your diet a few days before you start and after you finish your cleanse. But first, make sure you check with your doctor if dietary changes are appropriate for you.

STEP ONE: CLEAN UP YOUR DIET

Before you start any cleanse, take the refined and processed foods out of your diet. That means eating less food from packages and way more from the produce section. Ideally, you want your pre- and post-cleanse period to last about as long as the cleanse itself. This prepares your body to safely receive the nutrients and starts the process of building better eating habits.

We follow the 80-20 principle in the pre- and post-cleanse phase: 80 percent of the good stuff and 20 percent of your favorite foods. This is measured by approximate caloric intake over the day, so if you are indulging in meat and dairy, you'll reach the 20-percent mark quite quickly. Focus primarily on the good foods and stay consistent, which is the biggest challenge most people face. Make sure you have access to lots of delicious recipes, either the ones in this book or ones that meet the guidelines provided below. We also make a list of the potential takeout places near where we live so that if we need to, we can pick up a quick meal that doesn't throw off our cleansing plans.

Here are some foods to remove or reduce in your diet before you start cleansing:

- Refined sugar products
- Processed and junk food
- Bread, pastry, and other food made with gluten-containing grains (wheat, barley, rye, kamut, and spelt)
- Processed soy products (soy milk, fake meat, etc.)
- Alcohol
- Coffee and other caffeinated beverages
- Recreational drugs
- Excess oil and fat, such as any fried food
- Milk, cheese, and other dairy products
- Meat, fish, and crustaceans

The easiest way to do this is by replacing the sugary, salty, fatty food with lots of fresh, colorful fruit and veggies, nuts, seeds, grains, and legumes—think whole-food plant-based meals.

Everyone is different. Some people are fine with just drinking liquids on their cleanse, while others need to include some plant-based solids. Both options are right! Cleansing is not meant to be a struggle. Do what feels right for your body. The better your experience feels, the more likely you'll be able to maintain your path of wellness and enjoy the healthy results of your cleanse. Here are the foods that you can build your meals around while on a cleanse:

- Vegetables
- Fruit
- Beans and legumes
- Gluten-free grains (brown rice, amaranth, millet, quinoa, buckwheat, teff, sorghum)
- Sea vegetables (nori, kombu, dulse, wakame, sea lettuce)
- Nuts and seeds (twenty to twenty-five a day or a couple of handfuls)
- Healthier oils (avocado oil, coconut oil, and sesame oil to cook with; flax-seed oil and hemp oil for condiments or in smoothies but not for cooking)

- Condiments (apple cider vinegar, coconut aminos sauce, coconut nectar, nut and seed butters like tahini, pesto, sea vegetable flakes, gomasio—a Japanese seasoning made of unhulled sesame seeds and sea salt)
- Herbs and spices

STEP TWO: BREAK A SWEAT AND HYDRATE!

Get your lymph moving, your skin sweating, and your lungs gulping detoxifying breaths for at least thirty minutes, four times a week. A lot of the time we feel tired and achy due to dehydration. Make sure that you are drinking at least 8 cups of water a day—this can include herbal tea.

STEP THREE: REDUCE STRESS

Stress impairs our bodies' ability to function optimally. Take some slow breaths, enjoy a yoga or meditation class, or make more time for your hobby. The challenge most people face is not scheduling their hobbies or passions, and so although we'd love to have all the time in the world, the busy modern lifestyle doesn't always allow for downtime. Schedule the time for your passions—it should be easy to be resolutely dedicated to downtime and relaxation.

DURING THE CLEANSE

The master key to a successful cleanse is planning. You have to set yourself up for success. Plan your meals for three days in advance and buy all of the groceries you will need. During the cleanse, you will be eating 100 percent whole food and plant-based. We also suggest blocking off the time you're cleansing on your calendar. This is an investment into your overall well-being, so make sure you set time aside for preparing your meals, for movement and sweating, and for mindfulness practices and relaxation. Sip a warm glass of water with a bit of lemon or apple cider vinegar and do some light stretching when you wake up each morning.

While you are on the cleanse, you should try to get at least seven hours of sleep every night to support healing and elimination. Make sure you are still drinking water throughout the day to wash out toxins as they are being shed from your body. The more water you drink and the more you sweat, the less likely you are to suffer from side effects as your body cleanses.

THE SUCCESSFUL CLEANSE

BEST PRACTICES

Here are our best practices and tips to make your cleanse more enjoyable:

- Probiotics will help replenish the friendly bacteria in your gut that are sometimes destroyed by antibiotics, chronic overeating, and eating food laden with toxins. Try to buy either the enteric-coated capsules or the human strain probiotics, but whatever you buy, make sure it is coming from a fridge in the grocery store.

- Make sure you're still getting enough fiber. Eat small plant-based meals throughout the day or add some chia seeds into your juices. The chia will support the microflora in your gut as well as strip toxins from your digestive tract. We like to drop the chia seeds in, and then leave the juice to sit for five to ten minutes. The juice almost turns into chia jelly!

- Have your first juice or smoothie when you would normally have break-fast, and then drink your juices every three hours. You can plan your day based on when you'd be having lunch, dinner, and going to sleep, so that your routine doesn't feel too broken. Don't forget to shake the juices and smoothies well and drink them slowly.

- Are you hungry between meals? That's normal, as you're disrupting your well-established relationship with food. However, the cleanse should not be a struggle, so if you're feeling a little peckish, then raw food is a good option. Fruit, vegetables, nuts, and seeds are all completely fine to have while cleansing. For example: eat a handful of unsalted almonds or walnuts, or a leafy green salad with apple cider vinegar dressing and an avocado, or you can soak some chia seeds in room-temperature water for ten minutes and enjoy some chia pudding. You can also add another cleansing-appropriate juice or smoothie if you are really craving a meal.

- Drinking water will cut your hunger, too. Have a nice big glass of lemon water—it will also hydrate you and give you energy.

- With all this juice and water, you may be craving something warm. Decaffeinated herbal teas are great to have while doing a juice cleanse. Burdock root, nettle, and dandelion teas are some teas we drink while cleansing. We also love the Cleanse Blend by Harmonic Arts.

- Some people have headaches on their first day of the cleanse, but these usually dissipate by the second day. If you find yours hasn't and you think it could be from cutting coffee out of your diet, have a shot of espresso rather than a full cup of joe. It should do the trick.

- You'll probably lose some water weight, but in all likelihood it will come back, so don't approach the juice cleanse as a diet. Approach your cleanse as a step to detoxify your body, to get your diet back on track, and to help break some not-so-great food addictions.

- If you feel like you can't finish a juice, then don't sweat it. Drink as much as you can. Your body will tell you when you've had enough.

- While cleansing, try dry body brushing or coconut oil pulling. Gently brush your body in small circular motions from the ankles up toward the heart, always upwards with the exception of your back, which you can slowly brush from the neck down. This will stimulate the release of toxins accumulated in the body and help the skin absorb nutrients better. Swish coconut oil in your mouth immediately upon waking to remove toxins that have built up inside your mouth.

- If you're ready to take another cleansing step, give hydrotherapy a go or practice yoga. Alternating hot and cold showers stimulates circulation, and yoga poses (bending, twisting, lengthening) will naturally release unwanted toxins from your body while also relaxing your mind during your juice cleanse. You may want to try traditional or infrared saunas, massage, or colonics.

- Cleanse with a friend—compare stories and support each other.
- One of the best small-space exercises you can do is rebounding. Rebounders are small trampolines that can easily fit under the bed. Jump up and down to get your heart pumping and your lymph flowing. It's like being a kid again. Or, if equipment isn't your thing, going for a walk will help, too.
- If you're searching for inspiration during your cleanse, there are a handful of movies we recommend you watch: *Cowspiracy*; *Fat, Sick and Nearly Dead*; *Hungry for Change*; *Forks Over Knives*; and *Simply Raw*.
- Finally, when you wake up the morning following your cleanse, be proud and applaud yourself for your juice cleanse accomplishment. Ease yourself back into your diet—cleansing is about maintaining a healthy lifestyle rather than crash course changes.

YOUR BODY WILL TELL YOU WHEN YOU'VE HAD ENOUGH.

CLEANSING REACTIONS

Any time you change your diet or lifestyle, there will be a period of adjustment. Your reactions will be very dependent on what your diet was like before you started your cleanse. Here are some common reactions to cleansing and how you can mitigate the symptoms:

Skin breakouts: These are a common reaction, as the skin is our biggest detoxification organ.

- **What to do:** Drink lots of water and watch that your fat intake isn't too high. You can also try a diluted tea tree oil solution (one quarter oil to three quarters water) topically.

Gas and bloating: These are common symptoms that come with changes in your diet, especially when you increase your fruit and vegetable (and consequently your fiber) intake.

- **What to do:** Make a tea from half a teaspoon of fenugreek seeds, half a teaspoon of fennel seeds, three or four slices of ginger, and a tea bag of peppermint (which has carminative, or gas-reducing, benefits). Also, take a quality probiotic.

Brain fog: A general fog is commonly caused by a lack of sufficient calories, or possibly withdrawal from sugar and caffeine.

- **What to do:** Make sure you're taking in enough calories.

Low energy or fatigue: This is also a common symptom when you reduce your caloric intake, especially if you are used to eating a lot of calories, sugar, or both.

- **What to do:** Make sure you are getting enough calories and that you are eating a well-rounded diet of fats, protein-rich foods, and fiber.

THE CLEANSE MEAL PLAN

A little structure always helps. Use our meal plan flow chart to help stay on schedule with your cleanse and get the best possible cleansing experience. Once you get into your flow, you can modify the schedule to what works best for you, but we recommend our meal plan to get you started on the right foot.

THE CLEANSE MEAL PLAN	AWAKE	BREAKFAST	MID-MORNING
DAY 1	500 mL of warm water with lemon or apple cider vinegar	Cleansing juice or smoothie	Simple Chia Cereal (page 185)
DAY 2	500 mL of warm water with lemon or apple cider vinegar	Cleansing juice or smoothie	Salted Maple Granola (page 191)
DAY 3	500 mL of warm water with lemon or apple cider vinegar	Cleansing juice or smoothie	Simple Chia Cereal (page 185)
DAY 4	500 mL of warm water with lemon or apple cider vinegar	Cleansing juice or smoothie	Salted Maple Granola (page 191)
DAY 5	500 mL of warm water with lemon or apple cider vinegar	Cleansing juice or smoothie	Simple Chia Cereal (page 185)
DAY 6	500 mL of warm water with lemon or apple cider vinegar	Cleansing juice or smoothie	Salted Maple Granola (page 191)
DAY 7	500 mL of warm water with lemon or apple cider vinegar	Cleansing juice or smoothie	Simple Chia Cereal (page 185)

LUNCH	MID-AFTERNOON	DINNER
Cleansing juice or smoothie and Spring Rolls (page 198)	Cleansing juice or smoothie	Cleansing juice or smoothie and Super Satisfying Vegan Pho (page 210)
Cleansing juice or smoothie and The Hummus (page 197)	Cleansing juice or smoothie	Cleansing juice or smoothie and The Almost Mac and Cheese (page 204)
Cleansing juice or smoothie and The Almost Sushi (page 212)	Cleansing juice or smoothie	Cleansing juice or smoothie and Collard Wraps with Pumpkin Seed Pesto (page 200)
Cleansing juice or smoothie and Spring Rolls (page 198)	Cleansing juice or smoothie	Cleansing juice or smoothie and The Chili (page 206)
Cleansing juice or smoothie and Broccoli Avo Crunch Salad (page 209)	Cleansing juice or smoothie	Cleansing juice or smoothie and Celery Root and Leek Chowder (page 216)
Cleansing juice or smoothie and The Almost Pad Thai (page 208)	Cleansing juice or smoothie	Cleansing juice or smoothie and The True Borscht (page 214)
Cleansing juice or smoothie and The Macro Bowl (page 207)	Cleansing juice or smoothie	Cleansing juice or smoothie and Vegan Cream of Asparagus Soup (page 215)

SUPERIOR AND MEDICINAL FOODS

Superfoods are considered the most nutrient-dense and bioactive choices available. They are often quite low in calories for their high vitamin, mineral, and phytonutrient content. There was never a need to identify superfoods until the food industry became flooded with so many low-nutrient processed foods, some of which actually contain anti-nutrients that rob the body of vitamins and minerals as you digest them. In the modern age, our society has become overfed and nutrient starved by a food industry that relies on shiny, feel-good marketing rather than quality ingredients. One way to reverse this is to start introducing superfoods into your diet.

When we eat, much of the energy in the food goes to waste. Some of it moves right through us because we are unable to access it, and some of it is used up to process the parts that we *can* access. Low-nutrient foods waste a lot of energy; much of what the body needs is used for digestion, and we end up left with lots of empty carbohydrates.

Much of the body's processing of food requires our friendly flora, or gut bacteria. If we treat our bacteria right with good dietary choices, we get more health benefits out of everything we eat and we buffer the not-so-good parts of our food, such as the potential pathogens food may carry or encourage. Feeding our friendly flora with the right stuff to make them strong is another value that many superfoods add.

Making superfoods a part of your everyday lifestyle is as easy as making a smoothie. Of course there are many other ways to add them into your diet, such as superfood baking, pancakes, oatmeal, soup, sauce, salad dressing, ice cream, dessert, hot tonic drinks, and so on, but the basic smoothie is often the best place to start. It offers an easy medium to get creative with. One of the best things about a smoothie is that by design it is easy to digest, with everything already blended up, so the body requires less energy to process it and the nutrient content is delivered more efficiently. If we make just one of our daily meals a superfood smoothie, we can guarantee our body the nutrients it needs to stay healthy and strong.

Getting started can feel like the toughest part, especially if you are on a budget. Many of the ingredients are more expensive than conventional foods. This is part of what keeps our society making bad food choices. But when you take a closer look, you'll see that not only will superfoods increase your potential longevity, you don't need that much of them per serving. Though the up-front costs can be intimidating, the reality is you can make a pretty darn good superfood smoothie for under $5. Of course the $20 smoothie is also possible if you want to go all-out with the most exotic superfoods and organic fresh foods you can find.

Our recommendation is to set aside a reasonable budget that suits your lifestyle to start filling up your superfood pantry. Then as you get going, you can always add new ingredients. You will notice that they last a while even if you are using them every day.

In order to get a handle on the growing list of superfoods, which can be overwhelming, we approached Yarrow Willard, clinical/master herbalist and co-visionary of the Harmonic Arts Botanical Dispensary, a business that pioneered making superfoods accessible. Yarrow broke down his top superfoods and their benefits.

ACAI

Acai is a fruiting palm tree that grows in the subtropical areas of Central and South America. The pulp of its small purple berries is one of the healthiest foods you will ever find. They are high in antioxidants, B vitamins, trace minerals, and many other phytochemicals. Other than its high antioxidant content, the acai berry's main claim to fame is helping with weight loss. Other reported benefits are skin health, immune support, improved digestion, improved mental function, increased energy, anti-aging effects, and a better sex drive. It can be consumed as a juice or powder (half a teaspoon is recommended), and it has a nice flavor that makes a good addition to most food or drink recipes.

ACEROLA

A small tree that produces a fruit that resembles the shape of a cherry, it is native to Central America, with the biggest plantings of it now in Brazil. The fruit is quick to mold and so is usually processed right away into juice, jelly, jam, and syrup for home use or spray-dried, freeze-dried, or concentrated into powder for commercial use. It is extremely high in vitamin C and antioxidants, and also contains many other vitamins and minerals. Many health benefits have been attributed to the use of acerola, including blood sugar balancing, immune support, metabolic issues, cancer prevention, anti-aging effects, better digestion, and heart health. Typically, half to one teaspoon of the powder is added to food or drink, though you can use more if you want to.

ALFALFA

This extremely deep-rooted plant pulls up nutrients from far below the surface and is naturally high in many essential vitamins and minerals, including vitamins A, D, E, and K, all the B vitamins, biotin, calcium, folate, iron, magnesium, potassium, and many others. It is very high in protein, especially if you use it in its dried form. Alfalfa is a natural cleanser and detoxifier both to the land it grows on and in our bodies. It has been shown to help reduce cholesterol and improve the overall digestive function of the gut. Alfalfa is easy to get into the body by adding the powder into smoothie or food recipes, and it can be added to herbal tea blends.

CAMU

Camu is a fruit tree native to the Amazon rainforest that resembles a cherry. Like many Amazonian fruits, it contains many active compounds, phytochemicals, and amino acids. Its main claim to fame is its high vitamin C content, thirty to fifty times that of oranges, meaning that a half teaspoon of the powder provides more than four hundred times the daily requirement. Camu is also high in many vitamins, minerals, bioflavonoids, and other phytochemicals. A quarter to a half teaspoon is the recommended serving, which can be added to food and drinks or taken with water.

CHAGA

This mushroom shows up as a symbiotic sclerotium (growth) that is found mostly on birch trees in the northern regions of our planet. It has been used for at least several hundred years in Russia and Eastern Europe and is well known and used extensively by indigenous people of northern Canada, northern Europe, and Siberia. As a superfood and medicine, chaga has gained popularity over the last ten years, mostly because of its heavily researched, famous anticancer and immunomodulating qualities. Chaga is also used as a potent antioxidant. Chaga has been shown to be anti-inflammatory, reducing pain sensations. Like other mushrooms, chaga must be prepared in a way that makes its compounds available for absorption in the body. Cut pieces of the mushroom can be lightly simmered as a broth or a decoction-style tea, prepared as a dual extract tincture, or prepared as a pre-extracted edible powder form. The tea has a nice flavor with hints of vanilla; it can be used as a base for smoothies, hot drinks, or soups. The tincture and powdered extract can be consumed on their own or added to food and drinks.

CHLORELLA

Chlorella is a single-celled algae that is cultivated in Taiwan and Japan. This superfood is rich in many phytonutrients including amino acids, chlorophyll, beta-carotene, potassium, phosphorus, biotin, magnesium, zinc, and B vitamins. Chlorella has been shown to have profound nutritional benefits for the body: its high chlorophyll content and diverse spectrum of phytochemicals have a deep ability to detoxify the body, so chlorella has been used specifically for heavy metal and radiation detoxification. Other benefits of chlorella as a food are stabilizing blood sugar and cholesterol, enhancing digestive health, weight loss, and immune support. Commonly, chlorella powder is taken in good amounts (one teaspoon to one tablespoon) for two weeks to three months as a whole-body system cleanse. It can be added to smoothies, food, or taken on its own with water.

COCONUT WATER

Coconuts have long been considered the most functional survival plant in the tropics. Much of this fame is due to coconut water, which hydrates the body far more efficiently than regular water. It contains five essential electrolytes and many amino acids and trace minerals, which are critical to proper hydration. Coconut water is ideal for athletes or those with low water and mineral consumption and high energy output.

CORDYCEPS

This mushroom is a parasitic fungus that grows on insects (look this up on YouTube . . . the videos will blow your mind). It has a long history of use in China and Tibet, but has also been used by indigenous peoples around the world. Cordyceps is specific for the respiratory tract, working as a bronchodilator. Heavily used by athletes, cordyceps helps get more oxygen into the cells and increases endurance. Cordyceps is extremely effective for relief from bronchial inflammation. It is well known to relieve exhaustion, night sweats, and sexual impotency, and it acts as a sedative. Cordyceps will stimulate immune function and has been shown to increase white blood cell production in the bone marrow. It has been used to promote cellular health, to regulate blood lipids, to increase both male and female fertility, and as an aphrodisiac. It is ideally consumed as a pre-extracted powder or dual extract tincture, and can be added to food or drink or taken on its own.

GOJI

Considered to be one of the most nutritionally dense berries on earth, goji berries are one of the most popular foods in Chinese medicine and have been used as food and medicine for thousands of years. They are native to the Himalayas, though they are now grown in many parts of the world. Goji berries are rich in bioflavonoids, vitamin C, B vitamins, iron, selenium, and many phytonutrients. They contain a diverse group of polysaccharides that have been shown to have a modulating effect on the immune system. Goji berries have also been reported to benefit digestion and brain and eye health, reduce inflammation, have cancer-prevention effects, and have other benefits. Goji berries have a pleasant taste and make a great addition to many food and drink recipes.

HEMP SEEDS (HEMP HEARTS)

Over the last few decades, there has been a big increase in the use of hemp seeds as a superfood—some even consider them to be the perfect food. Though the whole seed can be eaten, the seeds are more commonly hulled, hence the name

THE BOOSTERS

LUCUMA

MESQUITE

SPIRULINA

CINNAMON

SHILAJIT

MACA

CACAO

MORINGA

ASHWAGANDHA

GOJI BERRIES

BROWN RICE PROTEIN

"hemp hearts." Hemp hearts are mostly made up of easily digestible protein and essential fats (omega-3s and GLA, an omega-6). They also contain fiber, iron, zinc, carotene, phospholipids, phytosterols, vitamin B_1, vitamin B_2, vitamin B_6, vitamin D, vitamin E, chlorophyll, calcium, magnesium, sulfur, copper, potassium, phosphorus, and other phytonutrients. Raw hemp seeds provide a broad spectrum of health benefits, including helping with weight loss, increasing and sustaining energy, speeding recovery from disease or injury, lowering cholesterol and blood pressure, reducing inflammation, improving circulation, strengthening the immune system, and controlling blood sugar. They are a great addition to the diet as a snack food or added to other food and drink recipes.

INCAN BERRY, OR GOLDEN BERRIES

Though berry-like, Incan berries are not true berries; they are in the tomato family and are closely related to tomatillos. They contain vitamins A, B, C, E, and K, iron, calcium, fatty acids, and many other minerals, phytonutrients, and antioxidant compounds. Golden berries are now being used for weight loss, to help regulate blood sugar, to support the liver, kidneys, and immune system, to fight inflammation, and to prevent cancer. They pack a nice sweet, tart punch and make a great snack or superfood addition to food and drink recipes.

KALE

Kale is one of the most nutrient-dense foods on the planet. One serving of kale contains well over the recommended dietary amount of vitamins C, A, and K, and it is high in many other vitamins and minerals. Kale has many potent antioxidants and bioflavonoids that have been shown to lower cholesterol, lower blood pressure, and improve overall cardiovascular health, as well as support the digestive system, liver, and eyes, and help with weight loss and detoxification. Kale is readily available to add to the diet: eat it raw in salads, steamed, dehydrated as chips, or as a powder added to smoothies and food.

LUCUMA

This comes from a subtropical fruit native to Peru, Chile, and Ecuador. Often called "gold of the Incas," these yellow or green egg-shaped fruits have a dry, starchy, golden flesh. The pulp is pounded into a powder and has a distinct maple to slightly pumpkin-like flavor. Lucuma provides fourteen essential trace elements, including a considerable amount of potassium, sodium, calcium, magnesium, and phosphorus. It has a sweet flavor and a low glycemic index, and has been used to replace sugar in some recipes. It has antioxidant and anti-inflammatory properties, and can emulsify fats when used with oils. Lucuma powder may be useful for people with diabetes and other health issues. It can be added to any drink, and is good in many foods, such as smoothies, yogurt, granola, pudding, or pastry.

MACA

Grown in the mountains of Peru, maca is a member of the radish family that has gained much fame around the world. It is rich in B, C, and E vitamins, as well as a good source of calcium, zinc, iron, magnesium, phosphorus, and amino acids. Maca is widely promoted to improve sexual function in both men and women and to help regulate hormone balance in women through the menstrual years and into menopause. Many athletes take maca, as it can increase energy and stamina and support the adrenals during stressful training. Many maca users report it to be helpful in enhancing their mood and reducing anxiety and depression. It has a distinctly sweet malted caramel flavor with an ever-so-slight radishy finish and can be used in a variety of ways including drinks, food, and desserts.

MAQUI BERRY

The fruit of a 3- to 4-meter-tall tree native to Argentina and Chile. Also known as Chilean wine berry, maqui berries were traditionally fermented into a low-alcohol drink used to improve strength and stamina. Maqui is a vibrant purple and is rich in anthocyanin and other flavonoids. The berries are hard when dried, so they are most commonly added to food and drink recipes as a powder.

MESQUITE POWDER

Mesquite is an extremely hardy tree that helps prevent desertification in the areas where it grows. The bark has been used as a barbecue flavoring, though it is the powdered pods that are used as a superfood. Traditionally the pods were pounded into a flour by the first peoples in the area where it grows. Mesquite is high in protein, low on the glycemic index, and a good source of soluble fiber, B vitamins, lysine, and many minerals including calcium, iron, manganese, zinc, and potassium. It has a sweet, nutty caramel-type flavor and makes a great addition to raw and cooked food, blender drinks, ice cream, and pretty much anything you can think of adding it to.

MORINGA

Known as the "miracle tree," moringa is a softwood that grows in India and Africa. The leaves, pods, seeds, and roots all have nutritional and therapeutic benefits. As this is a deep-rooted tree, it brings up many nutrients from subsoils and contains approximately twenty types of amino acids, forty-six types of antioxidants, and thirty-six anti-inflammatory compounds, including a wide spectrum of vitamins and minerals. Moringa has four times the potassium of bananas, twenty times the iron of spinach, and eight times the protein of yogurt. Moringa has been used in ayurvedic medicine to treat over three hundred diseases. Traditional uses are to support immune function, digestion, detoxification, sleep, weight loss, childbearing years, and heart, liver, and kidney health. It is tasty and easy to use as a powder made from the leaves, making it a nice addition to upgrade the nutritional content of food and drink recipes.

MULBERRY

Mulberry trees grow wild and cultivated in many temperate regions around the world. Dried mulberries are a rich source of protein, B vitamins, vitamins C and K, fiber, potassium, manganese, magnesium, and iron. They contain many antioxidants, including anthocyanins and resveratrol, and contain other immune and brain-supporting compounds. Mulberry leaves, and, to a small degree, berries, have been used traditionally to treat blood sugar imbalances, as well as irritation, inflammation, and redness. Mulberries make a tasty snack food and are a nice addition to the superfood diet.

MULTI-MUSHROOM COMBINATIONS

When it comes to using mushrooms as a superfood or medicine, much of the research and clinical experience shows that they are more effective when taken as a multi-mushroom combination. As many of the superfood mushrooms contain similar chemistry, the combination gives a fuller spectrum of the polysaccharides, triglycerides, and other phytonutrients they contain. Synergistically they work together to enhance the overall immunomodulating potential and antipathogenic qualities that these healing mushrooms are most known for.

PINE POLLEN

With over two thousand years of use in Chinese medicine, pine pollen has a long history as a superfood. The pollen from all pine trees is edible and abundantly available for a two- to three-week window in the spring. It is extremely rich in phytonutrients, including many amino acids and steroidal building blocks that increase androgens and restore hormone health. Pine pollen is an excellent source of flavonoid groups, antioxidants, vitamins, and minerals. It is also the best source of plant based testosterone. It is a mild-tasting fine powder that needs very little processing, making it a nice addition to your superfood kitchen.

REISHI

Used as a superfood and medicine in China for over two thousand years, reishi has been considered a major symbol of health and longevity in traditional Chinese medicine. Research shows that it can be used therapeutically for cancer, immune system issues, cardiovascular and respiratory problems, and urinary tract symptoms. It is antibacterial, antiviral, antifungal, and an ACE inhibitor. It inhibits blood platelet aggregation, protects the liver, and protects the body from radiation. Reishi lowers blood cholesterol and other blood lipids, reduces allergies and asthma, and reduces autoimmune issues. Reishi calms the mind, reduces circular arguments, and aids in insomnia. Reishi should be prepared in a way that makes its compounds available for absorption in the body. This means the whole or sliced mushroom must be lightly simmered as a broth or a decoction-style tea, prepared as a dual extract tincture, or prepared in a pre-extracted edible powder form. The tea is slightly bitter but can be used as a base for smoothies, hot drinks, or soups. The tincture and powdered extract can be consumed on their own or added to food and drinks.

SPIRULINA

Spirulina is a single-celled blue-green alga (also known as cyanobacteria). It is 60 to 70 percent protein by weight, which is more than any other plant source of protein.

Spirulina is full of vitamins, including many of the B vitamins, C, D, A, and E. It is also loaded with minerals, including four times as much calcium as milk, and is a great source of potassium, chromium, copper, iron, magnesium, manganese, phosphorus, selenium, sodium, and zinc. There are many anti-inflammatory and antioxidant compounds in it, including GLA (omega-6), flavonoid groups, and pigments such as phycocyanin and chlorophyll. Spirulina supports areas such as immune system integrity, allergy response, cholesterol, blood pressure, blood sugar, anemia, radiation detoxification, and overall strength and endurance. As a powder, spirulina is easy to add to drinks and food, or it can be taken in tablet form with meals.

TOCOTRIENOLS (STABILIZED RICE BRAN)

Tocotrienols are a rich source of antioxidants including vitamin E and beta-carotene (precursor to vitamin A). Tocotrienols are high in B vitamins, folate, biotin, choline, inositol, and vitamin C, along with many minerals, such as calcium, potassium, magnesium, phosphorus, iron, zinc, manganese, copper, and iodine. It has a sweet, almost vanilla-like flavor that can be used in many drinks and desserts, on yogurt, granola, or other food, and in recipes where its emulsifying properties are useful for blending liquids and fats.

SUPERGREENS ARE CONSIDERED THE MOST NUTRIENT-DENSE AND BIOACTIVE CHOICE AVAILABLE.

TURKEY TAIL

This mushroom is found all around the world growing on dead trees. Turkey tail and its extracts are some of the most studied of all the superfood and medicinal mushrooms. In particular, it contains a glucan-protein complex of polysaccharide-K (Krestin, PSK, PSP) that is used in cancer therapy to counteract the immune-depressing action of chemotherapy. Approved in 1980 in Japan for use with chemotherapy, it is covered by all Japanese health care plans. Both the isolate and the whole mushroom have been shown to increase survival time of cancer patients. There has been great interest in its ability to work as an antiviral for HIV, HPV, hepatitis, and many other viruses. Turkey tail can be made into a decoction-style tea like other tree mushrooms and makes a nice addition to a multi-mushroom immune-supporting broth or tea. It can also be consumed as a pre-extracted powder or dual extract tincture and can be added to food or drink or taken on its own.

WHEATGRASS JUICE AND POWDER

The early stage grass of wheat contains high levels of phytonutrients and has been shown to have profound health benefits. Wheatgrass contains the whole B vitamin complex, as well as vitamins A, C, E, and K, and a wide spectrum of minerals, including calcium, cobalt, copper, iodine, iron, magnesium, manganese, phosphorus, potassium, selenium, sodium, zinc, and more than seventy trace minerals. There are also nineteen amino acids and over thirty beneficial enzymes in wheatgrass.

YACON

This is a large perennial plant that has been grown and cultivated for its tuberous roots in South America for thousands of years. The powder and syrup are commonly used as a healthy sweetener in various foods. Yacon is mostly made up of fructooligosaccharides, an indigestible form of fructose that doesn't cause sudden rises in blood sugar. Many people who have diabetes or are trying to lose weight find yacon beneficial because of its low caloric value and sweet taste. It has been reported to help lower blood lipid levels and prevent the accumulation of harmful cholesterol. Yacon is a great addition to any food or drink where you're looking for a sweet flavor without adding sugar.

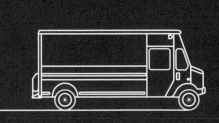

THE RECIPES

SMOOTHIES AND SMOOTHIE BOWLS

THE BLUEBERRY MATCHA

(anticancer, energizing, immune boosting)

Skip your morning coffee ritual. This antioxidant-packed smoothie is the perfect energizer to start the day. Matcha tea powder is an antioxidant powerhouse, packed with metabolism-boosting, cancer-fighting nutrients. Blueberries, tiny yet mighty, improve brain function. The cacao nibs add a subtle chocolaty crunch to the smoothie's texture.

Yields 16 oz

½ cup frozen blueberries
¼ tsp matcha tea powder
¾ frozen banana
1 Tbsp cacao nibs
1 tsp cinnamon
1 cup almond milk

Blend all the ingredients in a blender until smooth and creamy, then serve.

If the smoothie seems too thick, blend in a little more almond milk.

The health benefits of matcha tea exceed those of green tea because when you drink matcha you ingest the whole leaf, not just the brewed water. One serving of matcha has the nutritional value and antioxidant content of ten glasses of green tea.

THE GREEN SMOOTHIE

(antioxidant, cleansing, hydrating)

As the name suggests, this baby is green. Having a regular dose of greens is the most beneficial habit you could adopt. It's an easy habit to keep when your greens taste this good!

Yields 16 oz

2 kale leaves
Thumb-sized piece of ginger
¼ avocado
¾ frozen banana
1 Tbsp liquid chlorophyll
½ date
1 cup coconut water

Blend all the ingredients in a blender until smooth and creamy, then serve.

All hail kale! Per calorie, kale has more vitamin C than an orange, more calcium than a container of milk, and more vitamin A than any other leafy green.

If the smoothie seems too thick, blend in a little more coconut water.

For the all-green version, add ½ an avocado and take out the frozen banana.

Add chia seed, hemp seed, or flaxseed oil to add protein and essential fats (omega-3, -6, and -9 fatty acids).

THE AVOCADO PINEAPPLE

(healthy fats, hydrating)

If you like piña coladas . . . then you will definitely enjoy the Avocado Pineapple. A health-forward version of the popular bar drink. Just put the lime in the coconut and blend it all up.

Yields 16 oz

½ frozen avocado (scoop a half avocado out of its skin and put it in the freezer overnight)
2 cups cubed pineapple
¼ cup coconut milk
1 Tbsp coconut nectar
1 large squeeze of lime
A pinch of raw vanilla powder
3–4 ice cubes (we like to freeze coconut water)
Fill to 500 mL with coconut water

Blend all the ingredients in a blender until smooth and creamy, then serve.

THE GREEN PROTEIN

(anti-inflammatory, high fiber, high omega-3)

We drink this every morning (though you can of course drink it any time of the day). This smoothie checks all of the boxes for our daily needs.

Protein? Check.

Iron? Check.

Calcium? Check.

Taste? Check!

Yields 16 oz

1 cup spinach leaves

3–4 kale leaves

1 frozen banana

¼ avocado

1 tsp spirulina powder

1 tsp moringa powder

1 tsp ashwaganda

2 tsp flaxseed

1 Tbsp hemp seed

1 Tbsp chia seed

2 Tbsp almond butter

Fill to 500 mL with almond milk

Blend all the ingredients in a blender until smooth and creamy, then serve.

THE BLUEBERRY LAVENDER

(antioxidant, mineral-rich, stress reducing)

Light and refreshing. When you close your eyes and sip this smoothie, a relaxing aura of spring may overcome you. Lavender eliminates tension, relieves pain, and enhances blood circulation.

Yields 16 oz

¾ cup frozen blueberries

½ frozen banana

1 tsp dried lavender

2 peels of lemon zest

1 Tbsp chia seed

½ Medjool date

Fill to 500 mL with almond milk

Blend all the ingredients in a blender until smooth and creamy, then serve.

THE HEDGEHOG SMOOTHIE

(healthy fats, hormone balancing, mineral-rich)

When we were kids, Ferrero Rochers were our kryptonite. Needless to say, it was high on our bucket list to create a smoothie version. Our healthy, hazelnutty version packs in the flavor.
Yields 16 oz

½ frozen avocado (scoop a half avocado out of its skin and put it in the freezer overnight)
    (or substitute 1 frozen banana)
1 Tbsp cacao powder
2 Tbsp hazelnut butter
¼ tsp raw vanilla powder
½ tsp cinnamon
½ tsp maca
A pinch of Himalayan rock salt
Fill to 500 mL with almond milk
A few ice cubes or ½ cup of cold water

Blend all the ingredients in a blender until smooth and creamy, then serve.

THE HEARTY GREEN SMOOTHIE

(antioxidant, quality protein, mineral-rich)

Nut butters are our secret ingredient to make almost any smoothie taste creamy, rich, and smooth. If we want to step up the greens in a smoothie, we often balance the palette with a scoop of nut butter. Swap the almond butter for hazelnut or cashew butter to change up the flavor of this hearty smoothie!

Yields 16 oz

1 cup chopped collard greens
½ cup spinach leaves
¼ avocado
½ cup frozen cherries
½ tsp cinnamon
Thumb-sized piece of ginger
2 Tbsp almond butter
1 Tbsp hemp seed
Fill to 500 mL with almond milk

Blend all the ingredients in a blender until smooth and creamy, then serve.

THE STRAWBERRY COCONUT

(antioxidant, healthy fats, mineral-rich)

Where we grew up, there was this strawberry-Oreo milk shake that was all the rage at the corner shop. When we first opened, our goal was to recreate this drink, but of course we had to make a healthy version. We always aim for flavor and nutrition, and this smoothie hits the spot on both fronts.

Yields 16 oz

1½ cups halved strawberries
¾ frozen banana
1 Tbsp cacao nibs
¼ cup chopped coconut meat (or shredded dried coconut)
1 tsp vanilla extract
½ Tbsp coconut nectar
¾ cup of coconut milk
Fill to 500 mL with coconut water

Blend all the ingredients in a blender until smooth and creamy, then serve.

A LOOK INTO THE MIND, ITS EXPECTATIONS, AND THE SIMPLICITY OF MEDITATION

By Carolyn Anne Budgell, meditation guide and lifelong student

Yoga and meditation surprised Carolyn Anne Budgell when she was a nineteen-year-old ski bum. It initially helped increase her agility and calmness for her snowboarding, skateboarding, and trail running. Now, as a teacher in Vancouver, British Columbia, she continues her path to learn how to connect with others and feel at home in her skin. To Carolyn, the magic of yoga is that it grows quieter—toward a place where the physical, the internal, the spectacle, and the witness are all one. Her passion for silent meditation in forests is thanks to American spiritual teacher and author Adyashanti and the teacher, healer Michelle St. Pierre.

I am often approached by curious people about meditation (what the practice entails, their level of readiness to attend a workshop with me, the immediate benefits for them). These people tend to fall into two categories:

The timid, skeptical, or worried "novice" meditator who believes that meditation is too hard and probably too out there for them.

The whimsical or fiercely enthusiastic meditator who believes that meditation is simple and will surely provide everlasting bliss.

We are wired to have pre-established expectations. I believe that the above two outlooks on why meditation appears hard or easy come from what we've seen on TV or heard from others. Here are just a few of the distorted ideas about what a meditation practice or retreat looks like: gathering at sunset every night draped in white robes and chanting monotonously for hours into a blazing fire; retreating into the forest for months of silence without electricity or heat; forgoing meat, sugar, dairy, and alcohol and sitting in a personalized meditation room each morning for one hour. Whether or not you too have secretly believed in one of the above scenarios, remember that meditation is a unique, personal journey. Sometimes it's hard, sometimes it's wonderful, but above all it provides you with insight, a pause for reflection, and more awareness of the present moment.

Here are some of the benefits of meditation:

- An opportunity to pause, listen within.
- Quieting anxious thoughts.
- Reflection on the mind, the self, a topic, breath, or a visualization.
- Training the mind to focus, to be content, and to relax.

Meditation brings more awareness to everyday life. Rather than aiming for perfect contentment permanently, meditation is the means to live every aspect of life with more clarity and more awareness of thoughts, reactions, and how we connect with others: while walking down the street, in conversation with a friend, working on a project, washing the dishes, making a smoothie . . .!

Whether you are experienced with the practice or are brand new and intrigued about releasing stress, sleeping better, or improving your digestion, please remember that there is no one right way to practice meditation or mindfulness (that's perhaps why hundreds of schools and lineages exist—explore and find one that suits you!) and embrace a beginner's mind without expectations each time you sit, take a deep breath, or your mind spirals down the rabbit hole.

Now, for the best part: *how* do I meditate?

- Sit on a cushion or a chair, close your eyes, and count fifty breaths as you imagine your body relaxing with each exhale.
- Lie down with your legs bent and feet flat on the floor. Place your hands on your lower abdomen and visualize all the body parts that are touching the ground (set a timer for five or ten minutes).
- Go for a walk. Walking meditation is done with a very slow pace, hands in one position, mindfulness of your breath, no eye contact, awareness of all sounds, and no destination in mind.
- Meditate with a smartphone app or YouTube video, join a group in your city, take a workshop (nice for experienced meditators also, to learn new techniques), or get to a yoga class early and spend five extra minutes sitting or lying down while consciously breathing.

THE ALMOST CHOCOLATE

(energizing, high protein, hormone balancing)

Since we launched in 2011, this has been our most popular smoothie. Perfect for those who are a little timid of anything labeled a "healthy" smoothie and for healthy smoothie seekers alike. Packed with energy-boosting, hormone-balancing superfoods, this is the closest thing to a vegan chocolate milk shake.
Yields 16 oz

1 frozen banana
1 Tbsp cacao nibs
1 Tbsp cacao powder
1 tsp maca
1–2 heaping spoons of almond butter
1-2 Medjool dates
Fill to 500 mL with almond milk

Blend all the ingredients in a blender until smooth and creamy, then serve.

Add cinnamon, cayenne, or mint to spice up the flavor.

THE COCONUT OF COCONUTS

(energizing, healthy fats, hydrating)

A whole lot of coconut . . .

Yields 16 oz

¾ cup chopped coconut meat (or shredded
    dried coconut)
1 cup coconut water
2 Tbsp coconut cream
A pinch of raw vanilla powder
½ Tbsp coconut nectar
Large squeeze of lime
Fill to 500 mL with coconut milk

Blend all the ingredients in a blender until smooth
and creamy, then serve.

THE CACAO PEPPERMINT

(energizing, mood enhancing, healthy fats)

This energizing combination of cacao powder
and fresh mint leaves packs the punch of a
healthy After Eight mint. Full of greens, this
smoothie can be enjoyed all year long.

Yields 16 oz

1 cup spinach leaves
½ cup fresh mint leaves or ¼ tsp peppermint oil
1 frozen banana
½ avocado
1 Medjool date
1 Tbsp cacao powder
1 Tbsp chia seed
1 tsp maca
Fill to 500 mL with almond milk

Blend all the ingredients in a blender until
smooth and creamy, then serve.

THE BANANA BEET

(anti-inflammatory, athletic performance, quality protein)

A sweet, earthy smoothie with beets and hemp seed that is perfect for a light meal before exercise. Some have described this smoothie as an earthy cotton candy.

Yields 16 oz

½ beet
⅓ cup halved strawberries
1 cup spinach leaves
¼ avocado
¾ frozen banana
Thumb-sized piece of ginger
1 Tbsp hemp seed
Fill to 500 mL with almond milk

Blend all the ingredients in a blender until smooth and creamy, then serve.

THE GARDEN GREEN

(anti-inflammatory, liver supporting, high protein)

Green smoothies are one of the best (and easiest) ways to get all of your veggies into your daily routine. This one is packed full of greenery, just as if it came fresh out of your mom's garden.

Yields 16 oz

1 cup spinach leaves
1 frozen banana
1 cup torn romaine leaves
3 stalks parsley
3 stalks cilantro
¼ cucumber
Squeeze of lemon
½ apple
Thumb-sized piece of ginger
Fill to 500 mL with coconut water

Blend all the ingredients in a blender until smooth and creamy, then serve.

THE PUMPKIN PIE SMOOTHIE

(anti-inflammatory, antioxidant, mineral-rich)

When autumn is upon us and other folks are heading out to the farms in search of the elusive great pumpkin, switch things up and opt for this seasonal smoothie in place of its pie slice counterpart.

Yields 16 oz

⅓ 15 oz (425 g) can pumpkin puree, or fresh (about ½ cup)
¾ frozen banana
¼ avocado
1 Medjool date
¼ Tbsp raw vanilla powder
Shake of cinnamon
Thumb-sized piece of ginger
Fill to 500 mL with coconut milk or almond milk

Blend all the ingredients in a blender until smooth and creamy, then serve.

Make an impression by adding a little spiced rum or Irish cream.

If your smoothie is too thick, add a bit of coconut water or almond milk to the mix.

THE FOUNDATION OF OPTIMAL HEALTH: PROPER HYDRATION

By Jennifer Trecartin Brott, registered holistic nutritionist and orthomolecular health practitioner

Jennifer Brott is one of those people that lights up a room when she walks in. Beyond her contagious positivity, Jennifer brings a whole lot of knowledge on health and wellness. She's a registered holistic nutritionist who lives in Vancouver, British Columbia. Her education reinforced the connection between optimal wellness and the eating of whole foods. Jennifer has taken full advantage of the opportunity to study with leaders in the health care industry, including leading author Dr. Paul Pitchford and Dr. Brian Clement, director of Hippocrates Health Institute. Jennifer is always evolving and growing her own learnings and recently became a certified herbalist. She specializes in gastrointestinal, food tolerance, pediatric, and oncology nutrition.

Your body is made up mostly of water. Approximately 85 percent of your brain, 80 percent of your blood, and 70 percent of your muscle is water. Every cell in your body needs water to live. Water helps cushion your joints, carry oxygen and nutrients into all your cells, and regulate your body temperature, heart rate, and blood pressure.

You also need water to keep your metabolism working properly, but to do that, you need to maintain a certain level of water in your body (around 4 to 6 liters). If you don't keep that amount, your body will start to dehydrate. Think of your car. If the oil level gets too low, the engine will start to run rough. If you totally deplete the oil supply in your car, the engine will stop running. It's the same with your body.

We also often mistake thirst for hunger. Staying hydrated throughout the day can mitigate random waves of hunger and help prevent headaches. Lastly, drink water twenty minutes before your meal and try to avoid drinking water during your meal. Drinking during a meal dilutes the digestive enzymes that your body needs for proper metabolism. Wait twenty minutes after eating and you're good to go for your next drink of water! Here are some tips to get you started:

HOW CAN YOU INCREASE YOUR DAILY WATER INTAKE?

- Start the day with a cup of hot water with a good squeeze of fresh lemon. This will give your digestive system a real boost.
- Throughout the day have water constantly available; keep a water bottle on your desk so you can top up your glass, and carry a bottle of water with you when you are on the go.
- Eat plenty of fruit and vegetables. These have a high water content and will contribute to your daily water intake.

ARE YOU GETTING ENOUGH?

- Drink water even when you don't feel thirsty; by the time you feel thirsty your body has lost between 2 and 5 cups of water!
- A handy way to check if you are drinking enough water is to pinch the back of your hand while resting it on a flat surface. When you release the pinch, the skin should snap back into place. If your skin responds slowly, you are probably dehydrated.
- Check the color of your urine. The more transparent it is, the more hydrated you are. You should seek to produce urine that is very pale yellow, pale yellow, or straw colored.

ENJOY DOING A LOT OF EXERCISE?

- Drinking water before physical activity will help keep your heart rate and body temperature lower.
- Stay hydrated throughout your workout to avoid muscle cramping and fatigue.
- After your workout, for a quick recovery, drink some coconut water, which is rich in electrolytes and magnesium.

THE SWEET BEET

(antioxidant, athletic performance, quality protein)

This is great before a run or workout. Beets are nitrogen-rich, helping to increase the blood flow to the muscles, which means that you get more energy and better performance when you are working out. Keep this secret to yourself and show up your friends at the next group run.

Yields 16 oz

1 cup frozen strawberries
½ beet
2 Tbsp pomegranate seeds
1 Tbsp goji berries
1 Tbsp chia seed
1 Tbsp flaxseed
Thumb-sized piece of ginger
¼ tsp raw vanilla powder
Fill to 500 mL with almond milk

Blend all the ingredients in a blender until smooth and creamy, then serve.

THE FIGS AND YUMMY

(hormone balancing, mineral-rich, stress reducing)

Prepare for a glass full of delight. Close your eyes and allow the flavor profile in this smoothie to transport you. The perfect addition to lounging in the sun, it's also good when you're trying to recreate a tropical experience without the plane ride.

Yields 16 oz

2 Tbsp cacao
2 Medjool dates
2 dried figs
¼ tsp raw vanilla powder
½ tsp cardamom
1 tsp ashwaganda
½ pear
1¼ frozen bananas
1 tsp maple syrup
Fill to 500 mL with almond milk

Blend all the ingredients in a blender until smooth and creamy, then serve.

THE CREAMY GREEN

(healthy fats, high fiber, quality protein)

The banana and cashews create a thick, nutrient-packed smoothie! Have it as a smoothie or mix things up and add toppings like goji berries, shredded dried coconut, or granola to make it a smoothie bowl. Experiment and make it something new each time. Mango is a slightly sweeter alternative to frozen banana, and you can mix up any greens in place of the spinach or kale.

Yields 16 oz

1 cup baby spinach leaves
½ cup chopped kale
½ cup soaked cashews
½ avocado
¾ frozen banana
1 tsp vanilla
1 Tbsp maple syrup
1 tsp cinnamon
Fill to 500 mL with almond milk

Blend all the ingredients in a blender until smooth and creamy, then serve.

THE CREAMSICLE

(antioxidant, energizing, vitamin-rich)

Poolside summer vibes are only a smoothie away. Like most good smoothies, this one was born as a happy accident from experimenting in the kitchen. This smoothie is packed with beta-carotene, which is good for your eyes and even better for your taste buds.

Yields 16 oz

1 cup fresh carrot juice
½ cup diced cantaloupe
1 frozen banana
¼ tsp raw vanilla powder
1 Tbsp coconut nectar
1 Tbsp coconut cream
Fill to 500 mL with coconut milk

Blend all the ingredients in a blender until smooth and creamy, then serve.

THE DIABLO

(healthy fats, hormone balancing, mineral-rich)

Spice up your life! This smoothie pays homage to real Mexican hot chocolate, but instead of using evaporated milk, we get the creamy and fatty flavors and textures from the avocado. The hormone-balancing effects of real chocolate will have you blissed out as you enjoy the fiesta of tastes dancing the lambada in your mouth.

Yields 16 oz

¼ avocado
1 frozen banana
2 Medjool dates
2 Tbsp cacao powder
1 Tbsp cacao nibs
Thumb-sized piece of ginger
½ tsp raw vanilla powder (or 1 tsp vanilla extract)
1 shake cayenne pepper
1 shake cinnamon
1 shake Himalayan rock salt
Fill to 500 mL with almond milk

Blend all the ingredients in a blender until smooth and creamy, then serve.

THE ANTI-INFLAMMATORY POSTWORKOUT HEALER

(anticancer, antioxidant, high protein)

Turmeric, a superstar food in our books, is a time-tested ayurvedic ingredient, dating back thousands of years and celebrated for its anti-inflammatory benefits. Curcumin, the most active element in turmeric, helps your body block fat, while improving liver function.

Turmeric is also antibacterial, antiviral, and antifungal, helping strengthen your overall immune system and making it a great addition for daily use.

Yields 16 oz

Thumb-sized piece of fresh turmeric
1 Tbsp hemp seed
1 cup frozen mango cubes
Thumb-sized piece of ginger
1 Tbsp chia seed
¼ tsp raw vanilla powder
1 tsp coconut nectar
A pinch of cardamom
A pinch of sea salt
A pinch of black pepper
¾ frozen banana
1 Tbsp coconut cream
Fill to 500 mL with coconut water

Turmeric detoxifies the blood by producing enzymes that break down toxins in the body. This makes turmeric a great hangover cure!

Blend all the ingredients in a blender until smooth and creamy, then serve.

THE HYBRID

(anticancer, antioxidant, healthy fats)

To double the nutrients, add your own fresh juice to your smoothies. We love combining carrot juice with fresh almond or coconut milk.

Yields 16 oz

1 cup fresh carrot juice
1 Tbsp coconut cream
1½ frozen bananas
1 shake cinnamon
¼ tsp raw vanilla powder
1 Medjool date
Fill to 500 mL with almond milk

Blend all the ingredients in a blender until smooth and creamy, then serve.

THE SUPER BERRY

(antioxidant, high fiber, healthy fats)

Berries are some of the richest sources of antioxidants of all foods. These nutritional powerhouses help prevent damage done by free radicals; however, we need to eat a variety of fruit and veggies frequently to protect our cells. This smoothie is an antioxidant super-shot to infuse your cells with life-giving nutrition.

Yields 16 oz

½ cup frozen strawberries
½ cup raspberries
½ cup blueberries
1 Tbsp chia seed
1 Tbsp hemp seed
¼ tsp raw vanilla powder
½ frozen banana
Fill to 500 mL with cashew milk or almond milk

Blend all the ingredients in a blender until smooth and creamy, then serve.

Add basil or mint to mix things up.

THE HORMONE BALANCER FOR HER

(hormone stabilizing, sustained energy, vitamin-rich)

Keep things in balance! Packed with all the things to keep your hormones where they should be—fibers, saturated fats, essential fatty acids, and superfoods. The serving of maca in this smoothie helps women maintain healthy hormone production, especially during pre-menopause.

Yields 16 oz

1 frozen banana
1 cup baked (or canned) yam
2 Tbsp hemp seed
1 Tbsp sesame seed
2 tsp maca
1 Tbsp chia seed
1 tsp MCT oil
2 tsp spirulina
1 shake cinnamon
Thumb-sized piece of ginger
Fill to 500 mL with coconut water

Blend all the ingredients in a blender until smooth and creamy, then serve.

THE HORMONE BALANCER FOR HIM

(hormone balancing, longevity, stress reducing)

This smoothie was built for men who are on the go and need to recharge their batteries. Designed with ingredients that encourage healthy aging and enhanced physical and mental health, this elixir is packed with adaptogens that work to regulate your endocrine system (hormone-producing organs) and help reduce the harmful effects of the modern lifestyle.

Yields 16 oz

1 cup frozen blueberries
5-7 frozen strawberries
½ avocado
1 Tbsp shilajit powder
1 Tbsp pine pollen
1 tsp maca
2 shakes cinnamon
¼ tsp raw vanilla powder
1 tsp ashwaganda
1 Tbsp coconut nectar
Fill to 500 mL with almond milk

Blend all the ingredients in a blender until smooth and creamy, then serve.

YOGA

By Alex Mazerolle

Alex is an entrepreneur and yoga teacher in Vancouver, British Columbia. She is a woman on a mission to help women come together and rise. Alex is a practitioner of real talk and is inspired by the transformative power of movement and all things nature.

You might think yoga is just for bendy people, or "#blessed" people, or people who pose on mountaintops once they've summited a small local hike. You might think yoga isn't for you and that the trend will pass just like your achy back, your restless sleep, or your busy brain. Well, take everything that you know about yoga off the table for a moment and consider this: yoga is for you. Yoga is for everyone. Yoga without all of its bells and whistles could be just the thing for a sore back, a restless sleep, and a busy brain. Yoga could just be the holistic approach you need on a physical, mental, and emotional level to balance out the rest of your life.

Yoga is one of the best chameleons we have in this day and age. It has lasted thousands of years, which shows it's not just a fad, and millions of people worldwide practice it every day, including professional athletes, monks, kids, the elderly, and even Sting. (Sting!) Yoga can be gentle and relaxed or vigorous and heart pounding; there are endless styles, ways, and teachers to cater to your lifestyle. Yoga can be the one hour of your day that can feel like an amazing workout, a therapy session, a motivational speech, a safe space, and a community hub all wrapped into one. Yoga can clear your mind, stretch your body, and calm your nervous system. Between the focus on breath and the alignment of the body, yoga offers countless benefits that include gaining flexibility, improving strength, increasing blood flow, and helping drain the lymphatic system; you can boost your immunity while correcting your posture.

My advice is to try it and see for yourself. Yoga is so accessible these days through studios, apps, videos, and books that you're sure to find something that works for you. It might take time. Be patient. Keep going back. It might seem weird at first, but try to look past the crazy poses or the expensive leggings and see yoga for what it truly is—a practice of knowing ourselves more deeply; of honoring our bodies on a physical, mental, and emotional level; and of deep inner work.

THE MANGO LASSI

(anti-inflammatory, antioxidant, healthy fats)

When we traveled through India, we constantly sought out mango lassis. The lassi is a popular yogurt-based drink from India, packed with probiotics, drunk to help with digestion. It's traditionally a blend of yogurt, water, spices, and sometimes fruit. This is our dairy-free, healthy version.

Yields 16 oz

1 cup frozen mango chunks
Thumb-sized piece of ginger
¼ tsp raw vanilla powder
¼ tsp cardamom
¼ tsp fennel seed
1 shake cinnamon
3½ oz coconut yogurt
3½ oz coconut milk
½ frozen banana
1 Tbsp coconut nectar
Fill to 500 mL with coconut water

Blend all the ingredients in a blender until smooth and creamy, then serve.

Add turmeric to spice it up and add an anti-inflammation benefit.

THE TAHINI GREENY

(healthy fats, mineral-rich, quality protein)

The tahini makes this smoothie nice and creamy—sounds like the start of a great smoothie poem. Poetry aside, tahini is a paste made from sesame seeds. It is rich in minerals such as phosphorus, magnesium, potassium, and iron. Tahini is also a great source of calcium and methionine, which aids in liver detoxification. It is also a 20-percent-complete protein, which makes it a better protein source than most nuts. This smoothie was inspired by our juicetender Kylie Goldstein.

Yields 16 oz

1 cup spinach leaves
2 kale leaves
1 small handful of fresh mint leaves
2 Medjool dates
1½ Tbsp tahini
1 frozen banana
Fill to 500 mL with almond milk

Blend all the ingredients in a blender until smooth and creamy, then serve.

THE PREWORKOUT

(antioxidant, athletic performance, hormone balancing)

The dietary nitrates found in raw beets help reduce the "oxygen cost" during exercise, so this smoothie will help you output more effort for the same amount of breath. Packaged alongside a ton of anti-inflammatory plant-based protein, this smoothie is the perfect start to crushing your daily workout.

Yields 16 oz

½ raw beet
1 cup blueberries
1 frozen banana
1 Tbsp almond butter
1 shake cinnamon
1 cup spinach leaves
½ Tbsp maca
1 tsp moringa
1 tsp MCT oil
1 Tbsp coconut nectar
Fill to 500 mL with almond milk

Blend all the ingredients in a blender until smooth and creamy, then serve.

THE ATHLETE

(cleansing, healthy fats, quality protein)

This satisfying smoothie will pump you up. It is jam-packed with anti-inflammatory ingredients and complete plant-based proteins. The abundance of omega-3 fatty acids in The Athlete is essential to the health of your brain, joints, and skin. The soluble and insoluble fiber will help keep you regular and are food for your microbiome. Remember, your bacteria have to eat too!

Yields 16 oz

1 Tbsp cacao
2 Tbsp brown rice protein
1 tsp spirulina
1 Tbsp hemp seed
1 Tbsp chia seed
1 tsp flaxseed
1 cup spinach leaves
1 Tbsp almond butter
1 Medjool date
1½ frozen bananas
Fill to 500 mL with coconut milk

Blend all the ingredients in a blender until smooth and creamy, then serve.

THE WATERMELON SMOOTHIE

(antioxidant, anticancer, hydrating)

Who doesn't like watermelons? Watermelons are 92 percent water and are full of important electrolytes. This refreshing and mildly sweet smoothie is soaked with nutrients, packed with vitamins A, B_6, and C, lycopene, antioxidants, potassium, and amino acids. As watermelons are mostly water, you don't need to add much liquid.

Yields 16 oz

1½ cups fresh watermelon
½ cup frozen strawberries
¼ tsp raw vanilla powder
1 Tbsp coconut nectar
3-4 coconut water ice cubes
Fill to 500 mL with coconut water

Blend all the ingredients in a blender until smooth and creamy, then serve.

Add mint to make this minty fresh, or add fresh dragon fruit for a little extra something special.

THE ZUCCHINI CHOCOLATE CHIP

(high fiber, healthy fats, hormone balancing, high omega-3)

Not sure if you want breakfast or dessert? Here is your solution. Opening with a mild sweetness from the banana and following up with some comforting flavors from the cinnamon and vanilla, this smoothie can be enjoyed day or night.

Yields 16 oz

1 cup zucchini
1 frozen banana
¼ cup walnuts
2 Tbsp cacao nibs
1 shake cinnamon
¼ cup raw vanilla powder
A pinch of sea salt
1 Medjool date
Fill to 500 mL of almond milk

Blend all the ingredients in a blender until smooth and creamy, then serve.

Top with cacao nibs or chopped walnuts.

THE GINGER SNAP

(anticancer, anti-inflammatory, mood enhancing)

This smoothie is the taste of fall in a glass. The warming action of ginger will heat you from the inside out, and the savory pumpkin will instantly take you back to mom's homemade pie. This smoothie will kick-start your digestive fire and leave you satisfied.

Yields 16 oz

2 thumb-sized pieces of ginger
½ cup baked pumpkin or ⅓15 oz (425 g) canned
    pumpkin
¼ avocado
1 Medjool date
1 Tbsp cacao powder
Shake of cinnamon
¼ tsp raw vanilla powder
Fill to 500 mL with almond milk

Blend all the ingredients in a blender until smooth and creamy, then serve.

THE HYDRATING RECOVERY SMOOTHIE

(antioxidant, heart healthy, mineral-rich)

Prepare yourself for a glass of yum. This smoothie was designed to re-energize you after a good workout. It is packed with lots of antioxidants, vitamins, and minerals to help nourish your body. The natural fruit sugars will give you a boost after exertion, and the cooling action of mint helps promote healthy digestion.

Yields 16 oz

1 cup frozen blueberries
½ cup frozen strawberries
2 sprigs of mint
½ tsp raw vanilla powder
Fill to 500 mL with coconut water

Blend all the ingredients in a blender until smooth and creamy, then serve.

THE GLOW

(antioxidant, healthy fats, vitamin C–rich)

The best beauty routines are internal. Begin with nutrient-rich foods and fats that boost and balance hormone production, bringing healthy, clear skin to the surface. Borage oil is one of the best sources of GLA, an essential fat for glowing skin. Vitamin C is another contributor to healthy, glowing skin; it supports adrenal health and energy. Your hormones can balance much more easily when your adrenal glands are healthy.

Yields 16 oz

½ cup frozen blueberries
¾ frozen banana
½ orange
1 Tbsp coconut oil
1 Tbsp borage oil
1 Tbsp hemp seed
1 tsp camu powder
Shake of cinnamon
Fill to 500 mL with cashew milk

Blend all the ingredients in a blender until smooth and creamy, then serve.

THE GREEN MATCHA

(anticancer, healthy fats, high fiber)

Need a real pick-me-up? Look no further. This smoothie was created as a mood-enhancing meal replacement to boost your performance both mentally and physically. Matcha has the amazing ability to both enhance calm and boost your energy levels unlike coffee, which leaves you to crash after a couple of hours. Full of quality fiber and healthy fats, it's a meal in a cup.

Yields 16 oz

1 tsp matcha
⅓ cup chopped coconut meat or 2 Tbsp
    unsweetened shredded dried coconut
½ tsp cinnamon
1½ frozen bananas
1 cup spinach leaves
½ zucchini
¼ avocado
1 Tbsp flaxseed
1 Tbsp chia seed
1 Tbsp hemp seed
2 Medjool dates
Fill to 500 mL with coconut water

Blend all the ingredients in a blender until smooth and creamy, then serve.

THE BLUEBERRY BOWL

(antioxidants, high fiber, sustained energy)

Soak some oats in water overnight to make them extra blendable (steel-cut oats are our choice), then blend together this satisfying breakfast bowl in seconds. The base, made with blueberries and coconut nectar, is packed with antioxidant and anti-inflammatory benefits. To further boost your nutrient intake, top with goji berries, cacao nibs, chia seeds, or toasted dried coconut.

Yields 18 oz

2 cups frozen blueberries
1½ cups steel-cut oats, soaked overnight
¼ tsp raw vanilla powder
1 frozen banana
1 Tbsp coconut nectar (or maple syrup)
Fill to 500 mL with almond milk
Toppings of your choice: goji berries, hemp seeds, chia seeds, flaxseeds, roasted almonds

Blend all the ingredients in a blender until smooth and creamy. Add desired toppings and serve.

Move over, bacon and eggs! You're no longer needed for breakfast. Upgrade any of your chosen smoothies with extra frozen fruit or ice to increase the thickness. After blending, add some toppings, and all of a sudden you have yourself a smoothie bowl. Perfect as a meal replacement or a hearty snack.

THE DRAGON FRUIT BOWL

(antioxidant, high fiber, vitamin-rich)

Believe it or not, this vibrantly pink bowl is all natural. Thanks to the bright, almost fluorescent, color of pitaya, or dragon fruit, this bowl is almost too pretty to eat. Pitaya, which has a mild sweetness, is a great source of antioxidants, magnesium, fiber, and B vitamins, making this an ideal postworkout snack.

Yields 18 oz

2 packages frozen dragon fruit puree (we use Pitaya Plus) or 1 dragon fruit peeled and chopped
½ frozen banana
½ cup frozen strawberries
2 Tbsp hemp seed
¼ tsp raw vanilla powder
Fill to 500 mL with coconut milk
Toppings: bee pollen, goji berries, hemp seed, and manuka honey

Blend all the ingredients in a blender until smooth and creamy. Add toppings and serve.

THE NERVOUS SYSTEM

By Dr. Avtar Jassal

Dr. Avtar Jassal is a pediatric and pre/post-natal chiropractor in Vancouver, British Columbia, who focuses on maximizing the nervous system's ability to heal and adapt. He believes strongly in the healing capacity of the human body and its ability to handle stress when functionally optimal.

For over a hundred years, chiropractors have been teaching their patients about the importance of their spine and its connection to their health. These days, the majority of the public understands the chiropractor's relationship with the spine; however, if we look back to 1895 when Dr. D. D. Palmer first discovered chiropractic, it was a different story. D. D. Palmer asked an important question: when two people are sitting at the same table, eating the same food, breathing the same air, how can one person be sick and the other healthy? He built chiropractic on the premise of the tone or adaptability of a human body responding to its environment.

This is finally explained by the latest scientific evidence in the field of epigenetics. Epigenetics says that it is not in fact our genes that control our destiny but rather how our genes get turned on or off by our interpretation of our environment. Our environment can be broken down into our physical, chemical, and emotional world, or as many chiropractors teach—thoughts, traumas, and toxins.

It is our good or bad thoughts, traumas, and toxins that turn our genes on or off, thereby changing our expression of health or disease. The things we think about, eat, and physically do affect the way our body responds at every given second of our life. The body's response to our environment is complex and simple at the same time. The simplicity is that if the cells of the body perceive anything in our environment as stressful, the body activates a certain response mechanism called the *stress response* or *fight or flight response*. The complexity is that the fight or flight response causes increased blood pressure, increased blood sugar, decreased blood flow to the parts of the brain responsible for higher levels of thinking, increased cholesterol reduction, increased cortisol production, and altered emotional states. The interesting thing is that the body doesn't differentiate between physical, mental, or chemical stress: the same stress response activates. So eating a hamburger, thinking a negative thought, or running away from a barking dog all activate the same stress response!

One of the most powerful symptoms of stress is postural distortions or subluxations. These postural distortions, such as forward head posture, rounded or unlevel shoulders, or an upper back hump, cause people to become stuck in a stress response even when the original stress is gone. A subluxation is basically a stuck stress response that can't shut off, leaving a person functioning at less than optimal levels. This leads to them responding poorly to their environment, being unable to handle new stresses, and making poor behavioral decisions.

Chiropractors correct these stuck stress responses (subluxations), allowing the body to heal and therefore to adapt better to their environment.

If our nervous system responses to thoughts, traumas, and toxins lead to poor health, then the opposite must be true as well. Having positive thoughts, good physical activity, and healthy nontoxic food such as fresh fruits, vegetables, and juices actually stimulates the healing response. Food in particular is there not just to give us energy, but also to heal us because it stimulates the nervous system to engage the healing mode opposed to stress mode. Food can be our instant stress reducer if we choose right!

EATING A HAMBURGER, THINKING A NEGATIVE THOUGHT, OR RUNNING AWAY FROM A BARKING DOG ALL ACTIVATE THE SAME STRESS RESPONSE!

THE "HEDGEHOG" BOWL

(healthy fats, mood enhancing, quality protein)

A chocolate smoothie may not sound like the healthiest thing, but when it includes antioxidants from cacao as well as protein, iron, and omega-3 fats from the hemp seeds, this bowl will keep you fueled.

Yields 18 oz

2 frozen bananas
¼ cup hazelnuts (soaked overnight) or 1 Tbsp hazelnut butter
1 Tbsp hemp seed
2 Tbsp cacao powder
2 Medjool dates
1 tsp maca
Fill to 500 mL with almond milk
Toppings of your choice: sliced banana, chopped hazelnuts, and cacao nibs

Blend all the ingredients in a blender until smooth and creamy. Add desired toppings and serve.

THE GREEN SMOOTHIE BOWL

(cleansing, healthy fats, quality protein)

Green smoothies can sometimes taste like a freshly mowed lawn (and unless you're doing shots of wheatgrass, that's not the result you're looking for). Don't worry: the flavors are so balanced in this smoothie, you won't even notice all the nutrients you're sneaking in.

Yields 18 oz

1 frozen banana
½ avocado
½ cup frozen blueberries
¼ cup cooked quinoa (cooled)
1 Tbsp almond butter
1 cup spinach leaves
1 cup kale
1 tsp spirulina
¼ tsp raw vanilla powder
1 Medjool date
Fill to 500 mL with almond milk
Toppings of your choice: granola, goji berries, bee pollen, and sliced fruit

Blend all the ingredients in a blender until smooth and creamy. Add desired toppings and serve.

THE CLASSIC ACAI BOWL

(antioxidant, heart healthy, high fiber)

After traveling to Brazil when we were twenty-one, we came home obsessed with acai. In Brazil, it's a staple in every breakfast bowl. Acai promotes heart health, aids in weight loss, promotes healthy skin and healthy digestion, and boosts your overall immunity.

Yields 18 oz

2 packs or 7 ounces of frozen acai puree
1 frozen banana
½ cup frozen blueberries
¼ tsp raw vanilla powder
¼ cup halved strawberries
Fill to 500 mL with almond milk

Blend all the ingredients in a blender until smooth and creamy, then serve.

Top with goji berries, shredded coconut, granola, and your choice of berries.

JUICES

THE GREEN

(blood nourishing, blood sugar stabilizing, cleansing, immune boosting)

With this recipe, we recommend playing around and rotating your greens. Experiment with spinach, kale, Swiss and rainbow chard, collard greens, dandelion greens, beet greens, mustard greens, etc. Changing your greens will bring different health benefits and switch up the flavor, and you'll find one that stands out as your top choice.

This juice is naturally cleansing due to its high content of greens. Full of chlorophyll, the blood of plants, this juice nourishes our own blood without adding extra sugar. Keep the skin on the lime for extra antioxidants. A key nutrient in limes helps prevent infections, which helps you stay healthy during the cold and flu season.

Yields about 16 oz

1 cucumber
3 stalks of celery
3 kale leaves
2 leaves of Swiss or rainbow chard
1 handful of baby spinach
1 lime
3–4 sprigs of parsley

Pass all the ingredients through the juicer.

Kale is one of the most nutrient-dense plants that we can eat. The phytonutrients called isothiocyanates (ITCs) have been shown to help regulate detoxification at a cellular level, making kale an essential ingredient in every cleanse.

THE REMEDY

(anti-inflammatory, cleansing, mineral-rich, vitamin-rich)

Who doesn't need a remedy? We need one almost every day. Wheatgrass juice is one of the best sources of chlorophyll, plus it is an effective healer because it contains vitamins A, C, E, and K, as well as B complex vitamins. It is extremely rich in protein and contains 17 amino acids, the building blocks of protein. Not too bad for a grass, right?

Yields about 16 oz

1½ cups cubed pineapple
¾ cucumber
½ cup wheatgrass
5 sprigs of mint
Thumb-sized piece of ginger

Pass all the ingredients through the juicer.

THE PROFILE

(antioxidant, energizing, immune boosting)

This is one of the first juices that we came up with when we launched. It has a sweet mix of all of our preferred fruits with a gentle kick of ginger. Packed with vitamin C, this is a good go-to juice when you're feeling under the weather.

Yields about 16 oz

3–4 carrots
1½ cups cubed pineapple
½ apple
½ pear
½ orange
Thumb-sized piece of ginger

Pass all the ingredients through the juicer.

GRANDMA'S GARDEN

(antioxidant, high fiber, liver supporting)

This is our take on the classic savory vegetable juice, but instead of buying it in a can, you can enjoy it fresh! Chock-full of anti-inflammatory plant proteins and enzymes, your gut will thank you when you drink this health tonic.

Yields about 16 oz

2–3 medium tomatoes
¾ cucumber
½ bell pepper
2 stalks of celery
3 carrots
2 sprigs of dill
3 sprigs of parsley
3 sprigs of cilantro
A pinch of Himalayan salt

Pass all the ingredients through the juicer.

THE PINEAPPLE BEET

(antioxidant, athletic performance, vitamin-rich)

Beets are bursting with immune-boosting vitamin C, fiber, and essential minerals like potassium (which are essential for healthy nerve and muscle function) and manganese (which is good for your bones, liver, kidneys, and pancreas). Plus, if you're looking for the right boost for your next workout, look no further. Studies have shown that drinking beet juice before exercise helped people exercise up to 16 percent longer. It's said that the nitrates in beets turn into nitric oxide, which can reduce the oxygen cost of low-intensity exercise as well as enhance tolerance to high-intensity exercise. Boom! Drop a beet in that next juice you make!

Yields about 16 oz

1½ apples
½ beet
6 strawberries
1 cup cubed pineapple
Thumb-sized piece of ginger

Pass all the ingredients through the juicer.

Juicing and the Nervous System

By Dr. Genieve Burley

Dr. Burley is a multi-talented woman. A modern Jack (or Jill) of all trades. She's a registered yoga teacher, a certified personal trainer, a spinning instructor, and a prenatal chiropractic. Passionate about wellness and supporting her community in healthy, happy living, Dr. Burley brings an expertise in anatomy to her yoga teaching. She combines a deep scientific knowledge with ancient practices creating powerful evidence-based, holistic classes and treatments.

How can juicing affect the nervous system? I can think of hundreds of ways, but let's just list a few:

1. Juice, especially with green leafy vegetables, helps to alkalize the body, which fights many forms of chronic disease and provides the optimal environment for the immune system. The great news here is that most vegetables and fruits are alkalizing.
2. Juice provides essential vitamins and minerals that support the optimal functioning of the nervous system and its support cells. When the proper building blocks are available to make hormones and neurotransmitters, the nervous and endocrine systems work optimally.
3. When the stomach is under sympathetic stimulation, digestion is reduced and dysbiosis (loss of good bacteria and growth of bad bacteria) occurs. Cold-pressed juice provides an easily digested form of food for the intestinal lining to absorb with minimal work. Also, drinking juice provides good nutrition for the good bacteria to repopulate the intestines.
4. All vegetables and fruits in juice are full of water, and hydration helps the functioning of all cells in the body. Hydration will also help with constipation or diarrhea, both of which are common with chronic stress.
5. Juices are packed with antioxidants in the form of polyphenols. The polyphenols found in juice are protective against the neurodegenerative Alzheimer's disease when compared with vitamin supplements. If juice protects against

one neurodegenerative disease, there is plenty more research to do on the benefits of drinking juice three times per week.

Here are some tips on how to juice for nervous system health:

- Drink at least three vegetable-dominant juices per week.
- Choose juices that are high in nutrients but low in sugar. If you are doing a juice cleanse, the sweeter drinks are appropriate as they are calorically replacing solid food. But as a general rule, stick to the less-sweet juices.
- Drink water before and after drinking juice to get all the benefits of hydration. (Also, going to the bathroom will keep you more active!)

JUICE PROVIDES ESSENTIAL VITAMINS AND MINERALS THAT SUPPORT THE OPTIMAL FUNCTIONING OF THE NERVOUS SYSTEM AND ITS SUPPORT CELLS.

THE GREEN RECOVERY

(alkaline, anti-inflammatory, vitamin C–rich)

The perfect punch of nutrients for after a hard day's work, whether that be at the gym, on the trail, or just from running about. Turmeric and pepper team up to deliver anti-inflammatory benefits, orange keeps you feeling great with a healthy dose of vitamin C, while the kale and spinach keep your body in a blissful alkaline state. This juice was created by one of our juicetenders, Bruce Fulton. Bruce is a competitive boxer and rugby player and this is his go-to after any workout.

Yields about 16 oz

1 cup spinach leaves
1 cup kale leaves
2 thumb-sized pieces of ginger
¾ cucumber
Thumb-sized piece of fresh turmeric or 1 Tbsp turmeric powder
1 orange
½ lime
A pinch of black peppercorns

Pass all the ingredients through the juicer. If you're using turmeric powder, thoroughly mix in to your juice.

THE PINK MINT

(antioxidant, digestive aid, phytonutrient-rich)

The juice of perpetual summer! This is as refreshing as it gets; the combination of watermelon, lime, and mint will take you to beach-time bliss even on the grayest of winter days. Plus, mint is a quick and effective remedy for nausea, it promotes digestion, and it boosts your metabolism.

Yields about 16 oz

2½ cups watermelon chunks
1 lime
1 bunch of mint

Pass all the ingredients through the juicer.

THE SWEET GREEN

(antioxidant, mineral-rich, quality protein)

Want your greens and some sweetness too? This is the juice for you. The leafy greens and apple give this juice the balance that can please all spectrums of juice drinkers, from beginners to savvy juice-drinking veterans. Rotate your leafy greens through kale, Swiss chard, spinach, romaine, and collards to mix this juice up!

Yields about 16 oz

2 apples
3 kale leaves
1 cup spinach leaves
½ cucumber
½ lemon
3–4 sprigs of mint
1 oz aloe vera juice
5 oz coconut water

1. Pass all the ingredients except the coconut water through the juicer.
2. Mix in the coconut water.

THE CLASSIC

(athletic performance, blood nourishing, mineral-rich)

Every juice bar has a rendition of this juice. It's the ABC of juices, or as we call it, The Classic. In our version, we kicked it up a notch with ginger and burdock root. Burdock helps detoxify your blood and promotes blood circulation, improving your skin and mitigating conditions like eczema. Cancel the ginger, and The Classic is a great juice for your kids or anyone who's a little wary of vegetables in their juice.

Yields about 16 oz

1 apple
5–6 carrots
½ beet
Thumb-sized piece of ginger
½ burdock root

Pass all the ingredients through the juicer.

YOU ARE DOING A GOOD THING FOR YOU. SPREAD THE JOY. DO A GOOD THING FOR SOMEONE ELSE TODAY. WITH KALE.

THE THAI GRRRRRR

(circulation improving, mineral-rich, quality protein)

Pressed into this juice is a nice blend of sweet and spice. Thai chili picks things up with a subtle heat while the pineapple brings it back down with a note of sweetness. The main component in chilies is a chemical called capsaicin, which is responsible for creating the intensity of the heat. Capsaicin helps lower blood sugar levels, improves heart health, boosts circulation, thins blood, and helps protect against strokes. Spicing things up does the body good.

Yields about 16 oz

¾ Thai chili
3–4 thumb-sized pieces of pineapple
¾ cucumber
¾ kale leaf
2 thumb-sized pieces of jicama
½ lime

Pass all the ingredients through the juicer.

THE PATIO

(antioxidant, digestive aid, mineral-rich)

This juice was designed for patio season. Inspired by the popular mojito, mint and blueberry give it a nice refreshing flavor palette. If you want a nutrient-dense cocktail, add a spritz of alcohol, and you can retox and detox at the same time.

Yields about 16 oz

1 cup frozen blueberries
1 large pear
1 lime
Large bunch of mint
4¼ oz water kefir, kombucha, or coconut water

1. Pass all the ingredients except the water kefir, kombucha, or coconut water through the juicer.
2. Mix in the water kefir, kombucha, or coconut water.

THE SPICY APPLE

(anti-inflammatory, digestive aid, antioxidant)

Sniffles and sore throats begone! This grown-up apple juice is a cold-kicking superhero. Ginger is one of the healthiest (and in our opinion most delicious) spices you can get. Ginger can help relieve digestive problems such as nausea, loss of appetite, and motion sickness, plus it is a natural anti-inflammatory, antibacterial aid. If you don't have fresh ginger, blend in some ginger powder after pressing your juice.

Yields about 16 oz

3½ apples
1 lemon
2 thumb-sized pieces of ginger
2 shakes cayenne
Sprig of rosemary (optional)

Pass all the ingredients through the juicer.

THE SWEET CITRUS

(anti-inflammatory, antihistamine support, digestive aid)

Start your day with a juice that supports digestion and decreases inflammation. The powerful enzyme bromelain is found in large quantities in pineapple. Apple, carrot, and ginger also create an energizing anti-inflammatory synergy. The mint cools it down and helps soothe irritable bowels.

Yields about 16 oz

5 thumb-sized pieces of pineapple
½ orange
½ pear
½ apple
3 carrots
Thumb-sized piece of ginger
4–5 sprigs of mint

Pass all the ingredients through the juicer.

Strain with ice if you prefer your juice cold.

Seasonal allergies alert! Mint also contains rosmarinic acid, which has been found to be effective in reducing seasonal allergy symptoms.

THE LIVER LOVE

(antioxidant, athletic performance, enzyme-rich)

Your liver needs some love today. With over 500 functions in your body, supporting the liver with nourishing food and juice is an essential way to maintain health and longevity. The herbs in this juice have an abundance of supportive antioxidants that help reduce inflammation and cleanse the liver. Make a toast to your liver; you'll be glad you did.

Yields about 16 oz

2 stalks of celery
½ cucumber
1 green apple
½ beet
½ bunch parsley
½ bunch cilantro
½ lemon
1 shake cayenne pepper

Pass all the ingredients except the cayenne pepper through the juicer. Mix in the cayenne, and serve.

THE ROOT GREEN

(anti-inflammatory, blood nourishing, liver supporting)

A nutrient synergy for cleansing the body while supporting phase 2 detoxification. Beets are a crucial ingredient for complete body cleansing. They contain phytonutrients called betalains which are detoxifying and full of antioxidants and anti-inflammatory compounds. Add ginger for more anti-inflammatory effect and kale for its high chlorophyll content, and you've got yourself a juice you can use as a daily detox.

Yields about 16 oz

5 carrots
½ beet
Thumb-sized piece of ginger
Thumb-sized piece of turmeric
3 kale leaves
½ cucumber
A pinch of black pepper

Pass all the ingredients except the pepper through the juicer. Mix in the pepper, and serve.

Mixing black pepper with turmeric makes the turmeric 2,000 percent as efficient at decreasing inflammation by making the phytonutrient curcumin more bioavailable.

THE SPICY BEET

(antioxidant, athletic performance, mineral-rich)

Calorie for calorie, garlic is one of the healthiest
ingredients you could include in your regular diet.
Though it may linger on your breath for a little
longer than you want, the benefits are worth it.
Packed with manganese, vitamin B_6, vitamin C,
selenium, fiber, calcium, copper, potassium,
phosphorus, and iron, garlic and ginger give this
vegetable-based juice a nice bite that your body
will appreciate long after you've drunk the juice.

Yields about 16 oz

6 carrots
½ cup spinach leaves
½ beet
Thumb-sized piece of ginger
1 clove garlic
1 tsp cayenne powder

Pass all the ingredients except the cayenne
powder through the juicer. Mix in the cayenne,
and serve.

THE YUMMY YAM

*(anti-inflammatory, enzyme-rich, mineral-rich,
vitamin-rich)*

Yams give juice a really nice smooth consistency, while the cinnamon and ginger add a
lovely warming spice. Yams are energizing and
contain vitamins B_1 and B_6. Cinnamon is loaded
with antioxidants, has anti-inflammatory
properties, and lowers blood sugar levels. That's
enough reason for us to add cinnamon into the
mix. To change things up, try blending coconut
cream or milk with this juice to make it extra rich
and creamy.

Yields about 16 oz

1 yam
3 carrots
1 apple
Thumb-sized piece of ginger
1 tsp cinnamon

Pass all the ingredients except the cinnamon
through the juicer. Mix in the cinnamon, and serve.

THE HERBAL GREEN

(antioxidant, heart healthy, quality protein)

Adding fresh herbs is the fastest way to instantly increase the nutrient density of your juice. Basil comes armed with nutrients called flavanoids that protect the cell structure of white blood cells from radiation and oxidation damage. It also has provitamin A, a powerful antioxidant that protects cardiovascular health by preventing oxidation of cholesterol (only after cholesterol has been oxidized will it build up in blood vessel walls). If you have space on your patio, try growing some fresh herbs to include in your daily juice or just grab a fresh bunch and throw them in your juices and smoothies.

Yields about 16 oz

1 cucumber
½ apple
3 kale leaves
½ lemon
4 sprigs of basil (can substitute mint or rosemary)

Pass all the ingredients through the juicer.

THE PROBIOTIC SODA

Water kefir is kombucha's less-talked-about cousin. It is a fermented beverage packed with beneficial bacteria and is surprisingly easy to prepare. It is cultured by introducing a SCOBY (symbiotic culture of bacteria and yeasts) into what is basically sugar water. The beneficial bacteria in the water kefir grains consume the sugar, and as they metabolize it, they produce a variety of beneficial acids, food enzymes, B vitamins, and more beneficial bacteria. This process of fermentation also reduces the sugar content of the drink. Water kefir, like most fermented foods, supports overall gut health and systemic wellness.

Yields 4 cups

2 Tbsp water kefir grains
4 cups dechlorinated water
¼ cup unrefined cane sugar

1. Culture all ingredients in a loosely lidded jar for 24 hours out of the fridge.
2. Strain out the kefir grains and add the liquid to a bail-top bottle and leave on counter for another 24 hours before refrigerating. (Warning: Do not leave the bottles out longer than 24 hours without checking their pressure—the built-up carbonation could cause a bottle to explode!)

ANTI-INFLAMMATORY PROBIOTIC SODA

Want to take your probiotic soda to the next level? Take your kefir base from the previous recipe and add the ingredients below to your bail-top bottle. Leave for 24 hours for the flavors to come through, and then return to the fridge.

1 Tbsp sliced fresh ginger
1 Tbsp sliced fresh turmeric
½ tsp cracked black pepper
3 one-inch strips of orange peel (without the pith)
2 cups water kefir (above recipe)

1. Close the bottle, leave out for 24 hours, then refrigerate.
2. Strain before drinking. Kefir will keep for a month or even two in the refrigerator, but will gradually lose effervescence.

THE GREEN APPLE

(iron-rich, high protein, vitamin-rich)

Sometimes your greens just need a bit of sweetness. This is the mix for you. Spirulina is a great addition: gram for gram, it may be the single most nutritious food on the planet. Spirulina grows in both fresh and salt water. It belongs to a group of bacteria called cyano-bacteria, which can produce energy out of sunlight through photosynthesis. It is packed with protein, vitamins B_1, B_2 and B_3, copper, and iron. It helps control blood sugar and can reduce blood pressure.

Yields about 16 oz

3 apples
1 cup spinach leaves
¼ cucumber
½ lemon (peeled)
1 tsp spirulina

Pass all the ingredients except the spirulina through the juicer. Mix in the spirulina, and serve.

JENN'S ORANGE MINT JUICE

(antioxidant, quality protein, vitamin C–rich)

Whenever we have down time between orders or find ourselves with rainy-day free time, our team plays around with recipes. This is where many of our ideas and menu items come from. This juice was designed by one of our managers, Jenn, and has become a staff pick.

Yields about 16 oz

1 cucumber
2 oranges
3 sprigs of mint
½ cup spinach leaves
1 cup chopped kale

Pass all the ingredients through the juicer.

THE SWEET AND SPICY

(antioxidant, blood purifying, quality protein)

Satisfy the spectrum of your taste buds with this well-rounded juice. The greens, particularly cilantro, have a blood-purifying effect and help eliminate heavy metals from your body. This juice is rich in minerals like potassium, calcium, iron, and magnesium. Adding vitamin C from the lemons allows your body to properly absorb the iron. Love it or hate it, your opinion of cilantro is thought to be genetically predisposed. If you are of the latter camp, substitute parsley or basil as great stand-ins.

Yields about 16 oz

2 chard leaves
3 kale leaves
4–5 sprigs of cilantro
1 lemon
1½ cups cubed pineapple
½ cucumber

Pass all the ingredients through the juicer.

THE CREAMY CARROT

(antioxidant, healthy fats, immune boosting)

You don't have to be a "wascally wabbit" to love this juice. Sweet and creamy, this delicious, deluxe carrot juice will infuse your body with the powerful provitamin A, beta-carotene. With daily intake, carrot juice improves your eyesight and nourishes the lining of your internal organs. The "carrot on a stick" from drinking this juice is you'll have eagle eyes and a happy stomach.

Yields about 16 oz

6–8 carrots
½ lime
2 Tbsp coconut cream

1. Pass the carrots and lime through the juicer.
2. Mix in the coconut cream (use a blender for a creamy consistency).

THE MINTY MELON

(digestive aid, mineral-rich, vitamin-rich)

The freshness of this juice jumps off the page. Melon has that mellow sweetness that you just want to get cozy with. The pear balances things out, while the mint gives it that nice refreshing aftertaste that hangs around long after the juice is gone. Mint also helps with indigestion, can help relieve aches and pains, supports healthy skin, boosts immunity, and helps beat stress and depression.

Yields about 16 oz

⅓ honeydew melon, peeled
1½ pears
4 sprigs of mint

Pass all the ingredients through the juicer.

THE NO BLOAT

(anti-inflammatory, digestive aid, energizing, immune boosting)

It's always the worst when a bloated stomach gets in the way of your day. The ingredients in this juice can really make a difference. Pineapple has helpful digestive enzymes, and fennel and ginger are two fantastic digestion-boosting foods. They combine to promote prebiotic gut bacteria, which help the gut deal with food more efficiently and ultimately reduce bloating.

Yields about 16 oz

2 cups cubed pineapple
1 apple
½ fennel bulb
2 stalks of celery
Thumb-sized piece of ginger
2–3 sprigs of mint

Pass all the ingredients through the juicer.

THE REFRESHER

(antioxidant, digestive aid, vitamin C–rich)

This delicious juice comes packed with a lot of vitamins and tastes divine. Red grapes are a rich source of flavanoids, which help raise the good HDL cholesterol. They also contain an abundance of antioxidants, which help prevent cell damage from free radicals caused by stress on the body. The mint sweetens this juice but also brings a gentle cooling sensation to your gut. This juice will give you the same revitalized feeling as a short cold shower: fresh, cool, and energized.

Yields about 16 oz

1–2 oranges
2½ cups red or purple grapes
½ lemon
4 sprigs of mint

Pass all the ingredients through the juicer.

THE TURMERIC TONIC

(anti-inflammatory, energizing, mood enhancing)

We love balancing sweet and spicy. This has warming ingredients with ginger, turmeric, and peppercorns. If you're feeling brave, add some cayenne to top things off. If you're feeling not so brave, add some coconut nectar or blend in some coconut cream to take the heat down a level. To experiment, blend these ingredients with a cup of ice and some coconut water and turn it into a smoothie.

Yields about 16 oz

2 thumb-sized pieces of turmeric
Thumb-sized piece of ginger
½ lemon
1 cup cubed pineapple
½ orange
3 carrots
A pinch of black pepper

Pass all the ingredients except the pepper through the juicer. Mix in the pepper, and serve.

YOU'LL BE LIKE AN INVIGORA-TING SPRING DAY WITH A SKY FULL OF PUFFY CLOUDS. SOME OF THEM SHAPED LIKE CABBAGES.

THE HOT CABBAGE

(antioxidant, quality protein, vitamin-rich)

When you juice a cabbage, it's like showing up to your beer-league hockey game with a couple of stars from the pro leagues: you know you're winning. Cabbage contains powerful phytochemicals called polyphenols that strongly support the prevention of degenerative diseases like cardiovascular disease and cancer. Cabbage is a secret weapon in your fridge; use it whenever you can.

Yields about 16 oz

½ purple cabbage
1 cup spinach leaves
2 kale leaves
¼ apple
½ orange
½ lemon
Thumb-sized piece of ginger
1 shake cayenne

Pass all the ingredients through the juicer.

THE ALL VEG

(antioxidant, quality protein, vitamin-rich)

Everyone can use more vegetables in their day, and this is the way to do it. If you don't have time to mow down a couple of pounds of fresh vegetables or missed your salad at lunchtime, we've got you covered. This recipe has your back, even when the rest of the day seems to have failed you. Add ginger, black pepper-corns, or cayenne to bring some spice to the mix or a pinch of Himalayan salt if you prefer things on the savory side. Rosemary, basil, or dill are also nice additions.

Yields about 16 oz

1½ cups spinach leaves
2 stalks of celery
4–5 carrots
½ red pepper
1 cup chopped kale
½ beet

Pass all the ingredients through the juicer.

Meet Your Microbes

By Desiree Nielsen, BSc RD (integrative registered dietitian)

Desiree is a registered dietitian, author, and ambassador for the good (for you) life. She believes eating well isn't just about nutrients; the foods we choose to eat can either break our bodies down over time or nourish our cells and restore our health and vitality. Desiree takes an integrative approach to nutrition and shares how the power of plant foods can transform and re-energize your mind and body.

Imagine a place where something invisible to the naked eye could rule its entire universe. Where something so seemingly insignificant could affect how that universe defends itself, sends global communications, and obtains fuel.

Now stop imagining and look in the mirror. Human, meet your microbial maker: the microbiota. You might know it as your intestinal flora, but this is no genteel country garden. The 10 trillion bacteria that live in you and on you (right now!) have the remarkable power to shape your digestive, nervous, and immune systems from their command center in the gut. Every day, they are fighting for territory, access to food, and control over their universe.

Your digestive tract is essential for processing and harnessing the nutrients from the food you ingest, but its importance to human health doesn't end there. In fact, roughly 70 percent of your immune activity occurs along and within the digestive tract. The bacteria that live in your colon have the remarkable ability to communicate with your immune system to help it operate more intelligently. The right bacterial mix means a calmly alert system, but allow the wrong bugs to get a foothold, and the sanctity of the gut barrier is diminished. Once that happens, the immune system responds by setting the place on fire: that's right, chronic inflammation can be the result of the wrong kind of bacteria thriving in your gut.

What's more, those same bacteria can interact with the nervous system found in the gut. You might not know this, but the gut is often called your second brain, and for good reason: it contains more neurons (nerve cells) than your spinal cord! And it's not always your first brain calling the shots; communication is a two-way street. Your gut is not Vegas, and what happens there doesn't necessarily stay there. Your microbiota can alter the levels of neurotransmitters such as serotonin (the "feel-good" neurotransmitter) and GABA (the "chill out" neurotransmitter) produced by your nervous system. In fact, there is a growing body of research that shows that the type of bacteria living in your gut can affect mental health, and links have been found between bacteria and depression, anxiety, and even autism.

We have a saying in my world: you are not what you eat, but what you digest and absorb. Well, our learnings about our microbial universe are augmenting that a bit. You are now also what your microbes digest and what *they* make you absorb.

Modern living seems hell-bent on messing with our microbial world. Diets filled with too many high-fat animal foods and sugar at the expense of fiber-rich plant foods foster the growth of the wrong kind of gut critters. Mental stress and inactivity affect the health of the gut and those living within it. The result? Something called dysbiosis—where the trillions of good guys get overwhelmed by opportunistic ne'er-do-wells that start wreaking microbial havoc: attacking the gut lining. Messing with digestive function. Inciting a chronic inflammatory response that may be more responsible for obesity and type 2 diabetes than we expected.

While you can't see the culprits, dysbiosis may be steering your ship in many ways, ranging from basic gas and bloating to irritable bowel syndrome or eczema. Getting the bugs right is critical to human health, so eat your greens, stop covering yourself in antibacterial hand sanitizer, and take a good probiotic to set a course for better health!

HUMAN, MEET YOUR MICROBIAL MAKER: THE MICROBIOTA.

NUT MILKS

THE ALMOND MILK

(anticancer, blood sugar stabilizing, energizing)

Equipment needed: *high-speed blender and a nut milk bag*

- **Add ½ cup of halved strawberries while blending the dates, salt, cinnamon and vanilla for a child-friendly snack.**
- **Add a tablespoon of cacao to make this "chocolate milk."**
- **Try using your almond milk with your coffee or tea.**

Almond milk is a diabetic's best friend. When eaten with a meal, almonds have been shown to help stabilize blood sugar levels. Almonds also increase the amount of antioxidants found in the body after consuming a meal. Both are important for improving health and preventing that after-lunch nap.

Yields 16 oz

1 cup raw almonds

3 cups water, plus more for soaking

2–4 pitted Medjool dates, to taste

½ tsp raw vanilla powder

1 Tbsp cinnamon

A pinch of Himalayan rock salt

1. Soak almonds in a covered jar for 8–12 hours. Drain and rinse. The purpose of soaking is for increased digestibility and creamier texture.
2. Blend soaked almonds with 3 cups of water on high for about 2 minutes or until smooth.
3. Place the nut milk bag over a bowl or pitcher and pour the almond milk mixture into the bag. Squeeze until all of the liquid is out.
4. Rinse the blender and pour the strained liquid back. Add dates, vanilla, cinnamon, and salt. Blend again. Store in a sealed container in the fridge for up to 3 days. Shake before drinking.

Almonds can be the first step to a healthier diet. According to the *British Journal of Nutrition*, adding almonds to a daily diet decreased the desire for refined and processed foods and animal proteins.

THE COCONUT MILK

(antibacterial, antiviral, metabolism boosting)

Equipment needed: *high-speed blender*

Coconut milk is rich, creamy, and delicious. We like to add it to smoothies, soup, or curry, or we just drink it on its own. It's also one of the least expensive milks to make, coming in at around $1 to make 2 cups. Coconut is packed with lauric acid and medium-chain fatty acids, which help kill bacteria, viruses, and fungi while boosting your metabolism. To add a little flavor boost, mix in vanilla, cacao powder, or strawberries.

Yields 16 oz

1 cup chopped coconut meat or unsweetened shredded dried coconut
4 cups water
1 tsp raw vanilla powder
1 Tbsp coconut nectar

Blend all the ingredients for 3–5 minutes or until creamy, and then seal in a container and chill in the fridge. Coconut milk has a shelf life of 3 days while refrigerated.

THE AUTUMN SPICED MILK

(anti-inflammatory, antioxidant, metabolism boosting)

Equipment needed: *high-speed blender*

When fall rolls around, it becomes all about pumpkin pie spiced lattes. This is our healthy, guilt-free version. Turmeric eases arthritis, fights inflammation, is packed with antioxidants, burns fat, and lowers cholesterol.

Yields 16 oz

1 cup homemade coconut milk (see previous page)

1 tsp turmeric powder or 1 Tbsp + 1 tsp juiced turmeric

¼ cup diced pumpkin or canned pumpkin

1 Tbsp coconut oil

¼ tsp cinnamon

¼ tsp nutmeg

¼ tsp raw vanilla powder

A pinch of black pepper

A pinch of sea salt

Thumb-sized piece of ginger

1½ frozen bananas

1 Tbsp flaxseed

1 Medjool date

Blend for 3–5 minutes or until creamy and then seal in a container and chill in the fridge. This seasonal drink has a shelf life of 1–2 days. It's best drunk soon after it's made.

THE CASHEW MILK

(bone building, calming, heart healthy)

Equipment needed: *high-speed blender and a nut milk bag*

Soak nuts in large batches, drain and dry, then place in the freezer for later use.

Cashew milk makes a great base for cream sauces and soups.

Cashews are full of magnesium, a mineral responsible for nerve and muscle function. This milk will give you good fats and energy, and promotes relaxation.

Yields 16 oz

1 cup raw cashews or 3 Tbsp raw cashew butter

3 cups water, plus more for soaking cashews

1½ tsp honey or coconut nectar

½ tsp raw vanilla powder

A pinch of Himalayan rock salt

1. Place cashews in a jar and cover with water. Soak for 4 hours. Drain and rinse.
2. Blend cashews or raw cashew butter with 3 cups of water for 2–4 minutes on high. If your blender can't break down the cashews to achieve a smooth texture, strain through a nut milk bag.
3. Add honey, vanilla, and rock salt. Blend again for 15 seconds. Store in a glass container in the fridge for up to 3 days. Shake before using.

Nut milk is the best way to enjoy the versatility of cow's milk without the dairy proteins involved (which are typically the cause of inflammation/allergic reactions). It tastes great and is humane, environmentally sustainable, easy to make, and easier on digestion. And did we mention it tastes great?

THE GREEN MILK

(anticancer, blood sugar stabilizing, energizing)

Equipment needed: *high-speed blender and a nut milk bag*

This one has two greats together: nut milk plus some choice greens. Packed with protein and chlorophyll, this is the best way to stay energized and full. It works as a meal replacement or after a good workout.

Yields 16 oz

1 cup raw almonds
1 cup spinach leaves
½ cup chopped kale
3 cups water, plus more for soaking
2 tsp lucuma
½ tsp raw vanilla powder
1 Tbsp cinnamon
A pinch of Himalayan rock salt

1. Soak almonds in a covered jar for 8–12 hours. Drain and rinse.
2. Place the soaked almonds, spinach, kale, and 3 cups of water in a blender and blend on high for about 2 minutes or until smooth.
3. Place the nut milk bag over a bowl or pitcher and pour the almond milk mixture into the bag. Squeeze until all of the liquid is out.
4. Rinse the blender and pour the strained liquid back. Add lucuma, vanilla, cinnamon, and salt. Blend again. Store in a sealed container in the fridge for up to 3 days. Shake before drinking.

THE GOLDEN MILK

(digestive aid, alkalizing, anti-inflammatory)

Equipment needed: *high-speed blender and a nut milk bag*

Our almond milk is blended with cold-pressed turmeric, cinnamon, cardamom, and raw organic honey. This milk is anti-inflammatory and antibacterial, cleanses the liver, and builds muscle and bone.

Yields 16 oz

1 cup raw almonds
3 cups water, plus more for soaking
3½ oz juiced turmeric or 1 Tbsp turmeric powder
1 Tbsp raw organic honey (we like manuka honey)
½ tsp cardamom
1 Tbsp cinnamon
A pinch of Himalayan rock salt

1. Soak almonds in a covered jar for 8–12 hours. Drain and rinse.
2. Blend the soaked almonds and 3 cups of water on high for about 2 minutes or until smooth. Add turmeric juice, honey, and spices and blend again.
3. Place the nut milk bag over a bowl or pitcher and pour the almond milk mixture into the bag. Squeeze until all of the liquid is out.
4. Rinse the blender and pour the strained liquid back. Blend again. Store in a sealed container in the fridge for up to 3 days.

THE BRAZIL NUT MILK

(glowing skin, immune boosting, metabolism boosting)

Equipment needed: *high-speed blender and a nut milk bag*

Brazil nuts are the crème de la crème of creamy nut milks. Jam-packed with vitamins, antioxidants, and minerals, Brazil nuts are a fantastic source of selenium, which protects cells from damage and can lower the risk of certain cancers. Brazil nuts also lower LDL cholesterol, the "bad" cholesterol.

Yields 16 oz

1½ cups Brazil nuts
1 tsp raw vanilla powder
1 tsp cinnamon
2 Medjool dates
3 cups water, plus more for soaking

1.   Soak Brazil nuts in a large bowl of water for 8 hours. Discard soaking water and rinse Brazil nuts.
2.   Blend the Brazil nuts, vanilla, cinnamon, Medjool dates, and 3 cups of water.
3.   Place the nut milk bag over a bowl or pitcher and pour the Brazil nut milk mixture into the bag. Squeeze until all of the liquid is out. Discard the pulp or set it aside for another use. Store in a sealed container in the fridge for up to 3 days.

THE HEMP MILK

(anti-inflammatory, weight loss aid, workout recovery)

Equipment needed: *high-speed blender*

Make sure to store your hemp seeds in the fridge or freezer. Because of the omega-3 fats they contain, the seeds can go bad quickly sitting on a shelf.

Did you know that hemp seeds can help you lose weight? Omega-3 fats are found in large amounts in hemp seeds. They help you digest and assimilate other fats and help decrease inflammation. Not only can you feel slimmer by adding hemp milk into your diet, it's also a great source of complete protein. Perfect for an after-workout anti-inflammatory protein shake.

Yields 16 oz

1 cup hemp seed
¼ cup walnuts
3 cups water
2½ Medjool dates or 1½ Tbsp honey
½ tsp raw vanilla powder
1 tsp cinnamon
A pinch of Himalayan rock salt

Combine all ingredients in a blender. Blend on high for 1–2 minutes, until smooth and creamy. Store in a glass container in the fridge for up to 3 days. Shake before using.

YOU'RE GETTING
STRONGER
JUST HOLDING
THE BOTTLE.
WORKING OUT
PROBABLY HELPS
A LITTLE TOO.
BUT MOSTLY IT'S
THE BOTTLE.

THE MEGA NUTRIENT MILK

(energizing, hormone balancing, workout recovery)

Equipment needed: *high-speed blender*

This mega nutrient milk is the perfect way to have a creamy and delicious nut milk before or after your workout without adding tons of sugar. The maca in the recipe helps balance your hormones and improves your mood. Lucuma, raw vanilla powder, and cinnamon all impart a sweet and delicious flavor to balance the bitterness of the hemp seeds. You can also make a mix out of all the dry ingredients to bring with you as a nutrient booster while traveling.

Yields 16 oz

1 tsp maca
1 tsp lucuma
1 tsp raw vanilla powder (or ½ tsp vanilla extract)
1 tsp cinnamon
2 Brazil nuts
¼ cup hemp seed
2 cups water or cold chaga tea
1–2 dates or 1 tsp coconut nectar (or to taste)
A pinch of salt

Blend together in a blender for 1 minute. Use as a nut milk or drink alone. Shelf stable for 3 days while refrigerated.

MAKE YOUR OWN NUT FLOURS

Now that you've made your own nut milk (congratulations!), you can save and reuse that beautiful fiber-rich, protein-rich nut pulp to make your very own nut flour for gluten-free baking. After you've squeezed all the liquid out of the pulp (make sure you get every last drop!), you can dehydrate the pulp and make your own flour.

1. On a dehydrator sheet (if you're using a dehydrator) or cookie sheet (if you're using an oven), spread the pulp evenly over the sheet.
2. Set the dehydrator to 115°F or set the oven to 200°F. Process the pulp for 4 hours in the dehydrator or 2 hours in the oven, or until the mixture has become completely dry.
3. Test for moisture by pinching the flour. If the flour leaves moisture on your fingertips or creates a ball from pinching, it still needs to dehydrate more.
4. Store in a glass jar, a BPA-free container, or other airtight container in the refrigerator for optimal freshness. Your homemade flour is shelf stable in the refrigerator for 3–6 months.
5. Use it in any gluten-free recipes or as a flour replacement.

WELLNESS SHOTS

THE TEQUILA OF WELLNESS

Immunity boosting, metabolism boosting, antibacterial, antifungal . . . this shot will keep you on your toes. One shot a day will keep the doctor away, but if you do come down with a cold, up your intake to a couple shots a day and you'll be back on your feet in no time!

Yields 3–4 oz (Serving size: 1–2 oz per shot)

1 lemon
2 thumb-sized pieces of ginger
Thumb-sized piece of turmeric
A pinch of black peppercorns
1 tsp flaxseed oil or hemp oil
½ tsp cayenne

1. Pass all the lemon, ginger, and turmeric through the juicer.
2. Mix in the peppercorns, oil, and cayenne.
3. Keep leftover shots refrigerated and they will keep well for 3–5 days.

To add an extra cold-kicking, bacteria-killing level to this shot, add 5–6 drops of oil of oregano.

THE DIGESTIVE

After a big meal, or if you just want to keep things flowing, this is the shot for you.

Yields 2 oz (Serving size: 1–2 oz per shot)

2 oz aloe vera water
5 drops of liquid chlorophyll
2 drops of peppermint oil

Mix ingredients together and enjoy! Keep left-over shots refrigerated and they will keep well for 5–7 days.

THE IMMUNITY BUILDER

We love the smoky flavor of shilajit. If lemon, ginger, and cayenne are the tequila of wellness . . . shilajit would be the Scotch. Add some cinnamon and coconut nectar to sweeten things up.

Yields 3–4 oz (Serving size: 1–2 oz per shot)

1 pea-sized amount of shilajit resin
½ tsp dual extract chaga mushroom tincture or powder

Mix ingredients with 1 cup of boiling water and then let cool to room temperature. Keep left-over shots refrigerated and they will keep well for 5–7 days.

THE FLU FIGHTER

Skip the pharmacy . . . tell the doctor you're fine. This is the shot when you're feeling a tickle in your throat and the flu is going around.

Yields 3–4 oz (Serving size: 1–2 oz per shot)

2 thumb-sized pieces of ginger
1 lemon
½ tsp cayenne
4–5 drops of an echinacea tincture

1. Pass the ginger and lemon through the juicer.
2. Mix the cayenne and echinacea into the juice.
3. Keep leftover shots refrigerated and they will keep well for 3–5 days.

THE ENERGY BOOSTER

No need for coffee. Knock this one back for a quick pick-me-up.

Yields 3–4 oz (Serving size: 1–2 oz per shot)

½ orange
1 carrot
1 tsp spirulina
1 tsp chlorella
5–6 drops of a ginseng tincture

1. Pass the orange and carrot through the juicer.
2. Mix the spirulina, chlorella, and ginseng into the juice.
3. Keep leftover shots refrigerated and they will keep well for 3 days.

CLEANSE JUICES

THE DEEP DARK GREEN

Kale to detoxify. Ginger to reduce inflammation and stimulate the immune system. The Deep Dark Green has us diving deep into feeling good. This nutrient-dense juice is our top choice for cleansing.

Yields about 16 oz

2 kale leaves
2 chard leaves
½ cup spinach leaves
¼ cup chopped broccoli sprouts
1 cucumber
½ lemon
4 sprigs of mint
Thumb-sized piece of ginger
10 drops of liquid chlorophyll

Pass all the ingredients except liquid chlorophyll through the juicer. Mix in the chlorophyll, then serve.

THE GREEN DIGEST-AID

Fennel is soothing on the stomach. Cabbage aids in better digestion and nutrient uptake. Ginger kicks things up a little. This refreshing, digestion-aiding juice is like an invigorating spring day with a sky full of puffy clouds. Adding kombucha gives this juice a nice refreshing, natural fizz.

Yields about 16 oz

½ apple
½ lemon
½ cucumber
¼ fennel bulb
¼ cup chopped cabbage
½ cup spinach leaves
4 sprigs of mint
Fill to 500 mL with kombucha

We like to use original, ginger, or mint-flavored kombucha.

1. Pass all the ingredients except the kombucha through the juicer.
2. Fill the juice to 500 mL with kombucha.

THE RED

Dandelion's phytonutrients reduce fluid retention. Its flavor helps increase digestion. Lemon stimulates the liver. There's a lot of power in yellow things. Ever see a lazy bee? Nope. Always busy.

Yields about 16 oz

½ apple
½ beet
4–5 carrots
3–4 dandelion leaves
3–4 chard leaves
4 sprigs of parsley
¼ cucumber
½ lemon

Pass all the ingredients through the juicer.

THE FULL VEG

This is our version of V8. You can really mix it up and throw in different vegetables, herbs, and spices. We've used dill in the recipe, but give cilantro, basil, fennel, or rosemary a try. The pinch of salt rounds this juice out with a nice savory kick.

Yields about 16 oz

1 cucumber
3–4 carrots
½ beet
½ cup spinach leaves
3 kale leaves
½ medium tomato
¼ medium yam
3 sprigs of dill
½ lemon
Thumb-sized piece of ginger
½ tsp Himalayan rock salt

Pass all the ingredients except for the salt through the juicer. Garnish with salt.

THE SKIN DEEP

Antioxidants from kiwis and strawberries. Apples to soothe your skin and reduce inflammation. Well hydrated, your skin will feel radiant and rejuvenated. This juice makes every day a good day . . . Even if it's Wednesday.
Yields about 16 oz

1 apple
1 cucumber
4 strawberries
1 kiwi
½ lemon
5 sprigs of mint

Pass all the ingredients through the juicer.

THE GARDEN OF EDEN

Cilantro is a grade-A detoxifier. The antimicrobial and chelation factors combat lead, mercury, and other heavy metal toxicity. Parsley is a good source of folate, which is one of the most important B vitamins and is also important for the health of your heart. Parsley is also rich in vital vitamins, including vitamins C, K, and A. Parsley keeps your immune system strong, strengthens your bones, and heals the nervous system. It also helps flush out excess fluid from the body and supports kidney function. But enough about parsley; this juice is garden fresh with its strong herb and spice profile. Green thumb not necessary—this one is 100-percent gardener approved.

Yields about 16 oz

½ apple
½ cup spinach leaves
¼ bulb fennel
¾ cucumber
5 basil leaves
3 sprigs of cilantro
3 sprigs of parsley
3 sprigs of dill
½ lemon
½ lime

Pass all the ingredients through the juicer.

THE SLEEP TONIC

This is the juice for sweet dreams! Romaine helps with restful sleep through a mild opiate-like chemical that it naturally contains. A little touch of mint soothes digestion and cleans your mouth, and some pear cools and regulates your digestive system.

Yields about 16 oz

1 cucumber
½ pear
1 head of romaine
1 lemon
5 sprigs of mint

Pass all the ingredients through the juicer.

SLEEP

By Dr. Eric Posen

Dr. Eric Posen is a wizard of wellness. With training from China and Canada, Dr. Posen is a naturopathic physician, chiropractor, and acupuncturist in Vancouver, British Columbia. He believes the key to treatment and healing is to not use a designated therapy for a condition, but rather to unravel how the patient's body can mend an illness on its own.

Perhaps the most sought-after experience for a human being, even before incredible sex or winning a lottery, is to have a good night's sleep. For 50 percent of us though, this is so elusive that we will spend a lot of our waking hours and resources trying to figure out how to get it. Why is it so difficult for so many of us to find the respite and restoration that a night's sleep can bring? Since sleep is a normal process in our lives, any problem we have with it reflects an imbalance in our overall mental and physical health. Body pains, nutritional deficiencies, toxic or allergic reactions, hormonal changes, emotional stresses, underlying diseases, and poor lifestyle choices all have a part to play in making sleep more of a nightmare.

We know quite a bit about what happens if we don't get enough good-quality sleep. For example, if you are a young to middle-aged adult, you require six or seven hours of good-quality sleep every night to be healthy. Regularly sleeping for more than eight hours or less than six will decrease your longevity. Other consequences may be depression, heart and cardiovascular disease, cognitive impairment, weight gain, and diabetes. In addition, we all know how we feel after a bad night, when our mood, attention, concentration, and stamina are all negatively impacted.

Why we sleep is a question that we have fewer answers for. We know that at night our brain clears all of the cellular garbage that built up during the waking day. In the morning, our brains are actually smaller, volume-wise, than when we went to bed. Also, as our brains use 20 percent of the oxygen and blood sugar that the rest of our body uses, it's thought that sleep restores the brain energy we expended during the day. It's also thought that we grow new nerve cells in our brain as well as shift short-term to long-term memory when we sleep, especially when we are in REM, or dreaming, sleep.

When we sleep well, we know it. We feel energized and alive. We look forward to what the day may bring. Good sleep resets every one of the mechanisms and rhythms within us that allow us to be healthy and present. Everyone knows that sleep is an essential human need, no different than eating and drinking, and yet many of us try to get by on less sleep. Making sleep a priority is just as important as making a healthy diet a priority. You need both to hit your optimal well-being. Obtaining enough quality sleep that's in tune with your body's natural internal clock plays a vital role in your mental and physical health. Make it a goal to hit seven or eight hours of sleep a night. You'll quickly see results in how much more alert and focused you are throughout your day.

AT NIGHT OUR BRAIN CLEARS ALL OF THE CELLULAR GARBAGE THAT BUILT UP DURING THE WAKING DAY.

THE FOOD

THE CHIA PUDDING

Do you remember chia pets? We never would have thought that those iconic indoor plants created such a nutrient powerhouse: chia seeds. Chia seeds are loaded with fiber, protein, omega-3 fatty acids, and various micronutrients. Chia puddings are one of the easiest snacks to make. We love them for breakfast, but they're great as a dessert or snack. We rotate our chia pudding flavors monthly in our store. Mix your chia up and play with ingredients from the sweet side to the savory side.

Serves 6 • Prep time: 10 minutes

Total time: 2 hours

Flavor Suggestions

Add to the base or cream, or try layering them:

Matcha

Mango

Acai

Passion fruit

Raw chocolate or cacao

Hazelnut

Chia Base

½ cup chia seed

3 cups almond milk

¼ cup maple syrup

1 tsp raw vanilla powder

¼ tsp salt

Chia Cream

2 cups soft tofu

½ Tbsp coconut oil

2 Tbsp maple syrup

½ cup coconut milk

¼ tsp raw vanilla powder

1. In a medium bowl, whisk together the chia base ingredients and refrigerate for 1–2 hours.
2. In a blender, combine all of the ingredients for the chia cream and blend on low speed until smooth.
3. Portion the chilled chia base into 6 containers and top with the chia cream.

THE FEED LIFE SIMPLE CHIA CEREAL

You will love the simplicity of this morning cereal. It's packed full of fiber, omega-3s, and protein. It travels really well, becoming more like a pudding as the chia absorbs the liquid, so throw it in a glass container and bring it to work. It also works great as a dessert: just add 1 tablespoon of coconut nectar to your milk, and it'll fill you right up.

Serves 1 • Prep time: 10 minutes
Total time: 10–15 minutes

2 Tbsp chia seed
1 cup hemp milk

Optional toppings (pick one or two or go crazy and add them all)
1 tsp cinnamon
1 apple or pear, chopped
¼ cup shredded dried coconut
2 Tbsp goji berries
½ cup fresh berries
1 banana, chopped
¼ cup chopped walnuts
¼ cup pumpkin seeds

1. Place the chia seed in a bowl.
2. Pour hemp milk over top and whisk until chia starts to absorb liquid.
3. Let sit for 10–15 minutes (in the fridge or on the counter).
4. Stir again and add toppings.

THE ALMOND BUTTER CUPS

Day in, day out, these deliciously vegan, gluten-free Almond Butter Cups are our number-one seller on the menu. Many of our regular customers buy them by the dozen. The only partnership better than peanut butter and jelly might just be cacao and almond butter. We guarantee these will be your new favourite treat.

Yields 12 cups • Prep time: 8 minutes

Total time: 30 minutes–1 hour

Chocolate Mixture

1 cup coconut oil

1½ cups cacao powder

1 cup maple syrup

Nut Butter Mixture

½ cup almond butter (or your preferred nut butter)

½ cup crushed almonds

¼ cup coconut sugar

Toppings (optional)

A pinch of Himalyan rock salt

12 almonds (1 per cup)

Cacao nibs

Edible flowers

Cayenne pepper

1. In a small pot, melt the coconut oil, cacao, and maple syrup on very low heat until the coconut oil is melted (don't let it come to a boil). Transfer to a small bowl and whisk thoroughly.
2. In a medium bowl, mix the almond butter, crushed almonds, and sugar and set aside.
3. Fill a dozen cupcake papers of a paper-lined muffin tin with about 1 teaspoon of the chocolate mixture. You can either brush, pour, or pipe the chocolate into the paper liners. Make sure the bottoms and sides are evenly coated with chocolate. Leave some of the mix aside for topping.
4. Refrigerate for 30 minutes or until hardened.
5. Once hardened, fill each cup with 1 teaspoon of nut butter mix.
6. Top each cup with the remaining chocolate mix (if the chocolate hardens, just reheat it) and put the cups back in the fridge for 10 minutes or until hardened.
7. Top the finished cups with the topping or toppings of your choice. Store the cups in the fridge or in a cool place until you're ready to eat them.

SO, WHAT EXACTLY IS FIBER?

By Jennifer Trecartin Brott, registered holistic nutritionist and orthomolecular health practitioner

Jennifer Brott is one of those people that lights up a room when she walks in. Beyond her contagious positivity, Jennifer brings a whole lot of knowledge on health and wellness. She's a registered holistic nutritionist who lives in Vancouver, British Columbia. Her education reinforced the connection between optimal wellness and the eating of whole foods. Jennifer has taken full advantage of the opportunity to study with leaders in the health care industry, including leading author Dr. Paul Pitchford and Dr. Brian Clement, director of Hippocrates Health Institute. Jennifer is always evolving and growing her own learnings and recently became a certified herbalist. She specializes in gastrointestinal, food tolerance, pediatric, and oncology nutrition.

Fiber has a very important role to play in the body. It is the indigestible component of whole grains, nuts, seeds, legumes, fruit, and vegetables. When eating a whole-food diet, it is recommended to consume 25–30 grams of fiber daily.

There are two main types of fiber in fruit and vegetables: insoluble and soluble. Insoluble fiber adds bulk to the stool, helps keep the bowels regular, fills you up, and speeds up the passage of food through the digestive tract. This type of fiber is mostly removed from juice, although it is still present in smaller amounts. Soluble fiber absorbs water like a sponge and provides bulking matter that acts as a prebiotic to support good bacterial growth and digestive health. It also regulates blood sugar, may lower blood cholesterol, slows the transit of food through the digestive tract, and helps fill you up.

As well as slowing down the absorption of sugar, it also slows down the absorption of nutrients. Some nutrients are attached to the fiber and pass through your system without ever being absorbed by your body. Juicing liberates these nutrients, separating them from the fiber. When you juice, you are extracting up to 70 percent of the nutrition right into your glass, and without the insoluble fiber, your body absorbs 100 percent of these nutrients.

When you remove the fiber from the produce, the liquid juice is absorbed into your bloodstream quickly. If you are only juicing fruits, this would cause a rapid spike in blood sugar, and unstable blood sugar levels can cause mood swings, energy loss, memory problems, and more! Keep your juice to as many vegetables as possible to avoid this. Fiber is also filling, and without fiber in the juice some people get hungry again quickly, so juice should be used more as a snack in between your main meals.

UNSTABLE BLOOD SUGAR LEVELS CAN CAUSE MOOD SWINGS, ENERGY LOSS, MEMORY PROBLEMS, AND MORE!

THE JUICE TRUCK'S FAMOUS GRANOLA

We love granola. Food-wise, it's like your one friend that never lets you down. Granola is there for you in so many ways: breakfast, grab-and-go snacks, trail mix for a hike, for the kid who's a picky eater, as a topping, or on its own. We use this granola in our smoothie bowls, parfaits, and chia puddings, with nut milk as a cereal, and of course, for the purists out there, on its own.

Yields 8 cups • Prep time: 20 minutes
Total time: 1 hour and 20 minutes

2 cups coconut ribbon
¼ cup currants
¼ cup hemp hearts
¼ cup chia seed
1 cup crushed walnuts
1 cup crushed almonds
½ tsp cinnamon
¼ tsp cardamom
¼ tsp raw vanilla powder or vanilla extract
¼ cup orange zest
1 tsp grated ginger
5 Gala apples, grated
1 cup maple syrup

1. Preheat oven to 300°F.
2. In a large bowl, combine all the ingredients.
3. Spread the granola mixture evenly on a baking sheet lined with parchment paper.
4. Bake for an hour or until all of the moisture has evaporated and the granola is lightly toasted. Once it's sufficiently dry, let the granola cool. Then crumble it and store in an airtight container.

THE QUICK AND EASY SALTED MAPLE GRANOLA

The Canadian kind of granola, perfect for breakfast or for a snack. This granola with a hint of maple syrup is perfectly paired with some fresh almond milk or coconut yogurt and topped with fresh fruit.

Yields 4 cups • Prep time: 15 minutes

Total time: 45 minutes

1 cup crushed almonds
1 cup pistachios
½ cup pumpkin seeds
½ cup sesame seed
½ cup buckwheat groats
½ cup chia seed
1 Tbsp grapeseed oil
2 Tbsp maple syrup
1 tsp cinnamon
½ tsp sea salt

1. Preheat oven to 300°F.
2. In a large bowl, mix all ingredients together.
3. Spread the granola mixture evenly on a baking sheet lined with parchment paper.
4. Bake for 30 minutes until all of the moisture has evaporated and the granola is lightly toasted. Once it's sufficiently dry, let the granola cool. Then break it up into small pieces and store in a glass jar in your fridge. Sprinkle on yogurt or over fresh fruit and enjoy!

THE CACAO COCONUT BAR

Creamy coconut layers with smooth chocolaty cacao, topped with a little extra coconut . . . because who doesn't like a little extra coconut? When the Juice Truck first launched, Zach's mother Sandy made all of the healthy treats. This was the original bar sold at the truck, and it remains one of the top sellers. This bar is a go-to for kids and those with a bit of a sweet tooth.

Yields 36 bars • Prep time: 1 hour

Total time: 3 hours

Chocolate Sauce
3 cups cacao powder
3 cups maple syrup
2 cups coconut oil
1 tsp salt

Coconut Spread
½ cup chopped coconut meat
½ cup maple syrup or coconut
    nectar
½ cup coconut oil

Base
3 cups walnuts
2 cups pecans
½ cup raisins
½ cup shredded dried coconut

Topping
1 cup finely shredded dried
    coconut

1. For the chocolate sauce, place all of the ingredients in a food processor and blend until smooth.
2. Pour the chocolate sauce into a medium bowl and set aside.
3. For the base, place the walnuts and pecans in a food processor and pulse until lightly crushed.
4. Combine all of the base ingredients with the chocolate sauce and mix well.
5. Spread the base mixture evenly on a baking sheet lined with plastic wrap. Place another layer of plastic wrap on top of the base, and with a rolling pin, roll out the mixture until even from all sides. Refrigerate.
6. For the coconut spread, place the ingredients in a food processor and blend until smooth.
7. Take the base out of the fridge and remove the top plastic layer.
8. Evenly distribute the coconut spread over the base.
9. For the topping, sprinkle the finely shredded coconut over top and lightly press into place.
10. Refrigerate for 2 hours or overnight before cutting.

THE ENERGY PROTEIN BALL

Bite-sized and full of punch, these energy balls are great for before the gym or for a snack to keep you fueled any time of day. For a change of pace, try out different nut butters. Cashew and hazelnut are good substitutes.

Yields 12 protein balls • Prep time: 6 minutes
Total time: 1 hour 20 minutes

Base

1 cup dates
¼ cup water
½ cup maple syrup
1 cup almond butter
1 cup carob powder
1 cup sunflower seeds
½ cup hemp seed

Topping

Finely shredded dried coconut

1. In a food processor, blend together the dates, water, and maple syrup.
2. Transfer the mixture to a medium mixing bowl, and using a large wooden spoon, mix in the almond butter, carob powder, sunflower seeds, and hemp seed until a firm mixture forms.
3. Refrigerate for an hour.
4. Using your hands, form the mixture into 12 balls, and roll the balls over a bed of finely shredded dried coconut or any topping of your choosing.

NUTRIENT-PACKED GUACAMOLE

This snack can also double as a quick and satisfying meal. If you feel like sharing, two can enjoy this as a meal on leafy greens, or serve it with crackers and fresh vegetable sticks and it'll serve four.

Serves 4 • Prep time: 10 minutes

Total time: 10 minutes

2 ripe avocados

½ white onion, finely chopped

½ cup chopped cilantro

½ cup grated zucchini (optional)

¼ cup grated carrot or carrot pulp from juicing (optional)

½ cup chopped tomato

2 cloves of garlic, crushed and minced

Juice of 1 lime

1 tsp sea salt

1. Peel and mash the avocados in a medium serving bowl.
2. Stir in the rest of the ingredients or blend on slow and serve.

TASHA'S GARDEN-FRESH SALSA

The best part of running our business is our regulars. They are our family. And like any good family, they're always keen to share their food recipes, their smoothie recipes, and of course a little insight into what they'd like to see on the menu. This recipe is from one of our first regulars, Tasha. We're huge fans of healthy dips, and once we tried this one, we had to include it on our menu.

Serves 2–4 people, depending on how much you like your chips and dip • Prep time: 10 minutes

Total time: 10–15 minutes

2 cups Campari tomatoes
1 bunch green onions
¼ white or red onion
½–1 jalapeño (1 makes it very spicy)
2 cloves of garlic
1 large handful cilantro
Juice of ½ lime
2 tsp white vinegar
½ tsp sea salt or to taste
Fresh pepper to taste

If you're not one for too much spice, you can use ¼ cup canned "tamed jalapeños" in place of the jalapeño for a mild version of the salsa.

1. Roughly chop the tomatoes, green onions, white or red onion, and jalapeño.
2. Put all the ingredients in a food processor and pulse until you reach a chunky consistency or your consistency of choice. Be careful not to process for too long or the salsa will become too liquid.

THE HUMMUS

It doesn't take long to make this creamy, salty, spicy, savory hummus spread. We eat it with celery and cucumber sticks or crackers most of the time, but it's also delicious wrapped up in a collard green with some sprouts and veggies. We also use it instead of salad dressing or on steamed greens and quinoa. This dip is protein packed, nutrient dense and filling, the perfect on-the-go snack!

Serves 4 • Prep time: 10 minutes

Total time: 10 minutes

2 cups cooked chickpeas

2 cloves of garlic, crushed

1 tsp sea salt

1 tsp Moroccan spice or whichever blend of spices that you like (curry powder, Italian seasoning, and Tex-Mex are all great)

3 Tbsp lemon juice or orange juice

1 tsp apple cider vinegar

Place all your ingredients in a blender or food processor and puree until smooth and spreadable. Will keep in the fridge for 4 days.

Make this into a Mexican-inspired black bean dip by using black beans instead of chickpeas, adding 3 tablespoons pickled peppers or 1 tablespoon jalapeños, and adding ¼ cup of cilantro.

THE SPRING ROLLS

This bestseller at our truck and storefront is the perfect snack or meal to pack for a busy day at work. We are constantly selling out of these delicious and nutritious rolls because people love their portability and, simply put, they taste amazing. These ingredients for the rolls are a great start, but you can experiment with other raw and cooked vegetables to create different flavors and textures.

Serves 4 • Prep time: 20 minutes

Total time: 30 minutes plus 4–24 hours for marinating

From a 1-pound block of tofu, make 2 cuts lengthwise and four cuts crosswise to get 15 strips of tofu sized for this recipe. (You will have 7 remaining tofu strips. Refrigerate the leftovers and use for your next meal.)

When rolling your spring rolls, be sure to use ice-cold water.

Have fun experimenting with the ingredients. If you're feeling sweet, you can even make these spring rolls into a dessert by using fruits like strawberries and mangos with coconut yogurt as a dip.

Tofu Marinade

5 Tbsp soy sauce or tamari

5 Tbsp coconut aminos sauce

2 Tbsp coconut sugar

2 tsp grated ginger

2 tsp sesame oil

8 strips (½ inch each) of tofu (see tip for how to cut the strips)

Wraps

8 rice paper wrappers

Ice water

1 red pepper, cut into thin slices

1 bunch of cilantro

3 large carrots, shredded or grated

1 10 oz package of kelp noodles

Spicy Almond Dip

1 Tbsp fresh ginger

4 cloves of garlic

½ Thai chili

¾ cup almond butter (or smooth peanut butter)

2½ Tbsp coconut aminos sauce (or tamari or soy sauce)

1 Tbsp coconut sugar

2 Tbsp apple cider vinegar

½ tsp salt

1½ Tbsp miso paste

½ cup warm water

1. For the tofu marinade, mix all ingredients together in a bowl. Add tofu to your marinade mix and marinate for a minimum of 4 hours (maximum 24 hours) in a covered dish in the fridge.

2. For the wraps, wet the rice paper wrappers in the ice water until pliable (about 10 seconds). Shake off the excess water and let the rice paper sit for a minute before rolling.

3. For the dip, in a high-speed blender or food processor, blend all the ingredients until smooth and creamy. Adjust water and seasoning to reach desired consistency.

4. To finish the wraps, lay a rice paper wrapper on a clean surface and arrange the following ingredients on top: 1 strip of tofu, 3 red pepper slices, cilantro leaves, small bunch of carrots, and a topping of kelp noodles. Fold the wrapper away from you, followed by both sides, and continue to roll the wrapper until sealed. Set aside. Repeat with the other wrappers.

THE COLLARD WRAPS WITH PUMPKIN SEED PESTO

This is a great lunch for school or work. Gotta love autumn—that time of year when root vegetables are ready to be pulled. Turnips, parsnips, sweet potatoes, yams, beets, carrots—you get the idea. Make a big batch and save some for breakfast. It's easy to pack and stays fresh till the following day.

Serves 4 • Prep time: 15 minutes

Total time: 40 minutes

Collard Wraps

1 yam

1 turnip

1 sweet potato

1 parsnip

1 Tbsp coconut oil

1 tsp minced rosemary

1 tsp black pepper

1 tsp sea salt

1 bulb of garlic

4 collard green leaves

1 box or 4 oz broccoli sprouts

Pumpkin Seed Pesto

1 cup raw pumpkin seeds

1 cup chopped kale or spinach leaves

1 cup basil, cilantro, or parsley

6 cloves of garlic, minced

½ cup pitted kalamata olives

⅓ cup fresh lemon juice

2 tsp freshly cracked black pepper

1 tsp chili flakes (optional)

1. Preheat oven to 350°F.
2. For the collard wraps, chop all root vegetables (yam, turnip, sweet potato, and parsnip) into 1-inch cubes.
3. Drizzle coconut oil over the root vegetables, add the rosemary, pepper, and salt, and toss.
4. Cut the top off the garlic bulb so that little tips of skin are just showing and most of the outer husk has been removed. Wrap in tinfoil.
5. Spread the root vegetables on a cookie sheet and place in the oven with the garlic.
6. Bake for 20–30 minutes, checking frequently (every 10 minutes) and flipping the veggies as needed. When done, the root vegetables should be soft in the middle and have a nice crust on the outside. The garlic should be soft and spreadable.
7. Toss the garlic and roasted root vegetables together and set aside.

8. To make the pumpkin seed pesto, set a dry pan over medium heat.
9. Add the raw pumpkin seeds and stir frequently until they start to "pop" and get fragrant.
10. Remove from the heat. In the bowl of a food processor, add the pumpkin seeds together with the rest of the pesto ingredients. Pulse until everything is combined and the texture is crumbly. Set aside.
11. Lay out the collard leaves in front of you. Spread 2 tablespoons of the pesto along the spine of each leaf.
12. Distribute the root vegetables, garlic, and broccoli sprouts among the four leaves, and roll into wraps.

GOTTA LOVE AUTUMN. THAT TIME OF YEAR WHEN ROOT VEGETABLES ARE READY TO BE PULLED.

FOOD ALLERGY, SENSITIVITY, AND INTOLERANCE

By Dr. Katie Leah

Dr. Leah is a modern-day medicine woman, a natural healer who can remedy just about anything. She's also a licensed naturopathic physician in Vancouver, British Columbia. Dr. Leah believes diet, exercise, and lifestyle modifications are the main pillars of health and wellness. She has many naturopathic tricks up her sleeve and is skilled in a variety of therapies, including clinical nutrition and supplementation, herbal and homeopathic medicine, Chinese medicine and acupuncture, hands-on therapies (spinal manipulation, craniosacral, and fascial therapies), and injection and intravenous therapies.

Understanding the world of food allergies, sensitivities, and intolerances can be challenging. The symptoms are different for everyone and can range from being immediate and intense to delayed and subtle. If you think you have a food allergy or sensitivity, the first step is to find the right health care practitioner to help you navigate the process.

Identifying whether you have an allergy, sensitivity, or intolerance is important. Food allergies are caused by the body's immune system reacting to a particular protein found in a food like eggs, peanuts, or fish. In people who are allergic, these proteins are mistakenly identified as harmful and toxic. In response, their immune system releases antibodies and histamine, which cause reactions in the body that include swelling, hives, difficulty breathing, and anaphylaxis. True food allergies can be very serious and sometimes fatal, so be aware of these!

Food sensitivities and intolerances can be especially tricky to manage. Because they don't always cause an immediate reaction, they can also be harder to diagnose. Food sensitivities often start in the digestive system. Problems with the body's ability to digest and absorb certain nutrients properly may occur. Over time, they can trigger other changes to our body's natural flora. If you think you have a food sensitivity, here are some simple tips to try: be sure you are relaxed and sitting down while you eat, chew well, and include warm fluids or raw juices to help improve your digestive function.

The importance of a healthy, well-functioning digestive system cannot be over-stated. It forms the basis for the health of some of the most important organ systems in our body, including our immune, hormonal, and cardiovascular systems. The symptoms of an unhappy, unhealthy digestive system can be infrequent and are sometimes as mild as an occasional bout of discomfort following a meal. At worst, pain or discomfort can become a daily occurrence and can be severe enough to cause serious problems later on in life.

It is important to consider three things when you are dealing with any symptoms from mouth to bottom:

1. What are you putting in on a regular basis? Are you eating foods that you are sensitive to or intolerant of? Do you have the right mix of healthy, whole foods to provide you with the nutrients you need for optimal health?
2. How well are you digesting and absorbing these foods? Does your body have enough of the right enzymes and acids to do this well? Are you eating in a way that encourages this?
3. Is there something affecting your digestive ecosystem like yeast, parasites, or bacterial overgrowth? Do you have the right balance of healthy microor-ganisms to support your digestive system? Is there something that could be affecting this: medication, stress, or poor eating habits or foods?

If your digestive system is healthy and functioning well, it should hum away in the background like a well-tuned engine. When it starts to draw more of your attention because of regular pain or discomfort, get back to the basics of a clean, healthy diet full of seasonal fruit and vegetables; healthy proteins and fats; and whole grains, nuts, and seeds as you tolerate them. With the help of your health care practitioner, consider a short cleanse a few times a year to help reset your digestive system and give you a clean foundation on which to build your health.

THE ALMOST MAC AND CHEESE

We say "almost," but we like this recipe way better than its boxed grocery store namesake. This recipe is dangerously good. We recommend making an extra portion because we always want seconds and we're betting that you'll feel the same. This version of the classic comfort food offers all the flavor with none of the guilt. Plus, this meal is kid approved and very easy to put together for dinner if you don't have a ton of time.

Serves 4 • Prep time: 15 min

Total time: 45 minutes plus overnight soaking

1 cup cashews

3 cups carrots

2 cups cubed sweet potato

2 cups diced onions

1 cup nutritional yeast

1 clove garlic

1 cup roasted garlic cloves

1 Tbsp smoked paprika

1 tsp cayenne

Salt to taste

1 cup gluten-free pasta

1.   Soak cashews overnight in the fridge. If you forget to do this, a couple of hours will do, but they're best soaked overnight.

2.   In a medium pot, add carrots, sweet potato, and onions and enough water to cover. Cook until all vegetables are soft.

3.   Add cashews, nutritional yeast, garlic, roasted garlic, and all of the spices and use a hand blender on high speed until silky smooth. You can also transfer the ingredients to your blender, if you don't have a hand blender.

4.   Boil a gluten-free pasta or any pasta of your choice.

5.   Serve the sauce over the pasta. We always serve just a bit of extra sauce. Sauce makes everything better.

To roast garlic, put peeled garlic cloves into an oven-safe container. Add enough olive oil to cover the garlic, and add some salt and thyme. Roast at 350°F until the garlic is golden brown. Use the oil after as a garnish, in dressings, or on toast. Roast as much garlic as you want, but make sure you cover the garlic completely with oil, otherwise it will burn. Keeps well in the fridge for up to two weeks.

THE CHILI

Nothing screams "comfort food!" more than chili, and this recipe is no exception. We've also served this chili on brown rice or quinoa for extra protein, which makes it extra satisfying. This recipe freezes well, so don't be scared to double it and save the rest for later.

Serves 2 • Prep time: 20 minutes
Total time: 1 hour

When buying canned beans, buy them in BPA-free cans and run them under cold water for a minute.

Nut Crumble

½ cup walnuts
½ cup sunflower seeds
1 cup brown mushrooms
1 clove garlic, minced
1 Tbsp cumin powder
1 Tbsp coriander powder
1 Tbsp tamari or coconut aminos
    sauce (or soy sauce)
½ tsp pepper
¼ tsp sea salt

Chili

1 Tbsp grapeseed oil
½ tsp cumin powder
½ tsp chili powder
1 tsp coriander powder
½ tsp sea salt
½ cup diced red onion
2 cloves of garlic, minced
1 cup diced red pepper
1 cup diced zucchini
½ cup canned black beans
½ cup canned red kidney beans
1 cup chopped tomato
2 tsp date paste or maple syrup
½ cup chopped fresh cilantro

1. For the nut crumble, place all ingredients in a blender or food processor and pulse until crumbly.
2. Add the mixture to a pan over medium heat and cook until the mixture starts to brown. Set aside.
3. For the chili, in a large saucepan over medium heat, add grapeseed oil, cumin, chili powder, coriander, sea salt, and onions. Once onions become translucent, add the garlic, red pepper, and zucchini, and cook for another 10 minutes.
4. Add beans and tomatoes and drizzle in maple syrup. Let simmer for 15 minutes.
5. Add the nut crumble to the chili mixture and warm through. Garnish each serving with chopped cilantro.

THE MACRO BOWL

There are three macronutrients, or "macros": proteins, fats, and carbohydrates. All calories come from macronutrients (and alcohol). Vitamins and minerals, known as *micro*nutrients, are essential to your health, but they do not provide calories. Education aside, this is a straight-A salad packed with all three macronutrients and with great taste as well. It is consistently one of our top sellers.

Serves 4 • Prep time: 20 minutes

Total time: 1 hour

Toppings

2 cups yam cubes
2 cups tofu cubes
1 cup cashews
Grapeseed oil for roasting
Garlic powder to taste
Cayenne pepper to taste
Salt and pepper to taste
2 cups julienned carrots
2 cups julienned red cabbage
1 cup edamame
1 cup kimchi (vegan)
Sesame seeds for garnish
1 lime, cut into 4 wedges, for garnish

Dressing

½ cup almond butter
½ cup lime juice
¼ cup rice vinegar
¼ cup maple syrup
¼ cup coconut aminos sauce
¼ cup gluten-free soy sauce
½ Tbsp sesame oil
Cayenne pepper to taste
Salt and pepper to taste

Base

4 cups baby spinach leaves
1 cup cooked brown rice
½ cup cooked red quinoa

Making macro bowls with day-old rice is a good way to use up leftovers.

When roasting vegetables, consider making a bigger batch. Roasted veggies are a good go-to versatile meal option that can be used for many other recipes. Plus, they keep well in the fridge and can easily be reheated.

For dressings, use a mason jar for easy storage.

1. Preheat the oven to 350°F.
2. For the toppings, line a baking tray with parchment paper. Keeping the yam, tofu, and cashews separate, lightly toss each ingredient in grapeseed oil and spread it over the baking tray, keeping them separate. Season with garlic powder, cayenne, and salt and pepper to taste.
3. Bake until golden brown, then set aside to cool. For faster cooling, transfer the roasted vegetables to a cool plate and refrigerate for a few minutes.
4. For the dressing, combine the ingredients in a mason jar, add the lid, and shake until everything has been emulsified.
5. For the base, portion out the baby spinach between four bowls, top it with the rice and quinoa, and assemble the toppings around the bowl. Drizzle with dressing and garnish with the sesame seeds and lime wedges.

THE ALMOST PAD THAI

We love how this recipe has the perfect balance of sweet, savory, and spicy. Warming to the body and so satisfying, and perfect when time is at a premium. You'll be enjoying this pad Thai in just 20 minutes!

Serves 4 • Prep time: 10 minutes
Total time: 20 minutes

Not a huge fan of noodles? Substitute brown rice or raw spiraled zucchini.

Pad Thai

8 oz brown rice noodles (you can also use specific pad Thai noodles found in the Asian section at most grocery stores)
1 Tbsp grapeseed oil
1 tsp minced ginger
2 cloves of minced garlic
¼ cup shredded carrots
½ cup diced zucchini
⅓ cup thinly sliced purple cabbage (use a mandoline if you have one)
¼ cup crushed raw almonds or tamari almonds
½ cup chopped fresh basil
¼ cup finely sliced green onions

Sauce

¼ cup almond butter (raw is best but roasted works too)
2 Tbsp coconut aminos sauce or tamari
1 Tbsp maple syrup
Juice of 1 lime
2 Tbsp sesame oil
2 tsp Sriracha (optional)

1. For the pad Thai, bring a large pot of water to boil and prepare the noodles according to the instructions on the package.
2. For the sauce, in a small bowl, whisk together all the sauce ingredients and set aside.
3. Place a frying pan over medium heat and add the grapeseed oil, ginger, and garlic. Sauté for 3 minutes, being careful not to let the garlic burn.
4. Add the carrots, zucchini, purple cabbage, and the rinsed and drained noodles. Add sauce. Thoroughly mix together all the ingredients and cook for 5 minutes.
5. Once the noodles look slightly seared, remove the pan from the heat. Top each serving with almonds, basil, and green onions.

THE BROCCOLI AVO CRUNCH SALAD

This salad is a quick, tasty dish you're sure to make again and again. Let the salad sit for an hour in the fridge before serving to give the flavors a chance to mingle. The lemon juice is great for keeping the salad from browning.

Serves 4 • Prep time: 10 minutes

Total time: 15 minutes

Dressing

1 avocado

1 tsp sea salt

1 Tbsp lemon juice

2 cloves of garlic, minced

Salad

1 head of broccoli, chopped into florets

½ cucumber, chopped (peel it if it's not organic)

1 tomato, chopped

1 stalk of celery, sliced thinly

½ cup roughly chopped flat leaf parsley

¼ cup sunflower seeds

1. For the dressing, peel the avocado and mash until creamy.
2. Stir in sea salt, lemon juice, and garlic until combined, and set aside.
3. For the salad, mix together all of the ingredients except the sunflower seeds in a large serving bowl.
4. Pour the dressing over top and give the salad a good stir to coat the veggies in dressing.
5. Top with sunflower seeds and serve.

THE SUPER SATISFYING VEGAN PHO

Traditionally, pho, a noodle soup originating in Vietnam, is made by creating a broth that brews for hours. Our plant-based version is both delicious and quick to make. We make this dish during a cleanse to balance all of the raw food, juices, and smoothies we are having. Keeping with the theme of nutrient density, we've chosen to quickly blanch the veggies to prevent overcooking them and losing all of the nutrients.

Serves 4 • Prep time: 15 minutes
Total time: 40 minutes

Broth

10 cups vegetable broth (we suggest buying an organic, low-sodium version)
2 Tbsp grated fresh ginger
6 cloves of garlic, crushed and minced
2 tsp Chinese five spice powder (optional)
2 Tbsp coconut aminos sauce (or soy sauce or tamari)
1 cup dried shiitake mushrooms
1 cup sliced tofu or tempeh (optional)

Soup

1 Tbsp salt
1 cup sliced carrots
1 cup broccoli florets
4 heads of baby bok choy, chopped
1 cup thinly sliced cabbage
10 oz pad Thai noodles (preferably brown rice)

Toppings

Lime slices
Jalapeño slices
2 cups fresh bean sprouts
2 sprigs of fresh basil
Coconut aminos sauce

1. In a large soup or stock pot, add all of the broth ingredients, except the shiitake mushrooms and tofu or tempeh, and bring to a boil. Let the broth simmer for 20 minutes. Add the dried shiitake mushrooms and the sliced tofu or tempeh to the broth and continue to simmer.
2. For the soup, prepare an ice bath for blanching the vegetables. Fill a large bowl or your sink with cold water and ice and set aside.

3.   Bring a large pot of water to a rolling boil and add 1 tablespoon of salt. The water should taste salty. Add your carrots to the boiling water. After cooking for 2 minutes, add the broccoli and bok choy. After another 1½ minutes, add the cabbage and cook for 1½ minutes more.

4.   Quickly take the veggies out of the boiling water and put them directly in the ice water to prevent them from cooking further.

5.   Once cool, pat the veggies dry and set aside.

6.   Add the noodles to the simmering broth.

7.   Once the noodles are soft, pour the broth into serving bowls.

8.   Add the blanched veggies to the bowls of broth. Add the toppings of your choice and enjoy.

THE ALMOST SUSHI

Everyone loves sushi. It's fun to eat and nutritionally a very complete food. Nori is full of protein and minerals, and it adds a salty and chewy element to each bite. The chili mayo adds a spicy and creamy note that will make your mouth and tummy smile at the end of the meal.

Serves 4 • Prep time: 40 minutes

Total time: 40 minutes

When working with nori, always keep the shiny side facing down.

Make sure you have a sharp knife for cutting the rolls.

Keep your hands wet when placing the quinoa to keep the sushi filling nice and sticky.

Add a layer of plastic wrap on the sushi roller to keep everything together during the roll out!

Dipping Sauce

⅓ cup soy sauce or tamari

2 Tbsp coconut aminos sauce

¼ cup maple syrup

Zest and juice from 1 orange

¼ cup water

1 Tbsp grated fresh ginger

1 bunch of scallions

Chili Mayo

½ one-pound package silken or medium-firm tofu

1½ Tbsp water

1 Tbsp olive oil

1 small ripe avocado

1 Tbsp seasoned rice vinegar

½ Tbsp plain rice vinegar

1 tsp Dijon mustard

½ Thai chili

A pinch of salt

Sushi

4 nori sheets

1 cup cooked quinoa

½ yam, roasted, in thinly sliced batons

1 red pepper, sliced

1 cucumber, cut in thinly sliced batons

½ leek, roasted and cut into slivers

1 ripe avocado, sliced

3 carrots, shredded

1 cup pea shoots

1. For the dipping sauce, blend all ingredients except for the scallions. Once blended to desired consistency, top with chopped scallions and set aside.

2. For the chili mayo, blend all the ingredients in a blender or food processor. Once blended to desired consistency, set aside.

3. For the sushi, place a nori sheet onto a sushi roller. Spread ¼ cup of quinoa across the lower half of the nori and top it with yam, red pepper, and cucumber. Top with a line of chili mayo, and then add some leek and avocado. Finish with a handful of shredded carrot and some pea shoots. Wet the top and bottom of the nori sheet and roll it away from you until the sushi roll is sealed.

4. Cut into 8 pieces. Repeat the same process with the other 3 nori sheets.

THE TRUE BORSCHT

There's nothing quite like a grandmother's soup . . . or in this case a babushka's soup! Juice Truck chef Alina Bobyleva, born and raised in Kazakhstan, moved to Canada at the age of 12 and brought a whole lot of delicious Eastern European cooking traditions with her. After becoming a red seal chef and a nutritionist, Alina combined her cultural upbringing with a passion for nutrition and plant-based cooking. We like to call this modern and healthy adaptation of grandma's best soup "the babushka's granddaughter."

Serves 8 • Prep time: 20 minutes

Total time: 45 minutes

1 cup roughly chopped cabbage
½ cup roughly chopped celery
1 cup roughly chopped potato
½ cup chickpeas (canned or
    cooked)
1 cup roughly chopped peeled
    eggplant
1 cup roughly chopped onions
1 cup chopped or julienned beets

½ cup chopped or julienned leek
1 cup chopped or julienned carrots
1 cup canned tomatoes, drained
½ tsp tomato paste
½ tsp coconut sugar
½ cup chopped fresh dill
2 cloves of minced garlic
Salt and pepper to taste

1. In a large pot, combine cabbage, celery, potatoes, chickpeas, egg-plant, and onions. Add enough water to cover the vegetables.
2. Bring to a boil, and cook until the vegetables are soft.
3. Blend with a hand blender until the mixture has a smooth consistency. If you don't have a hand blender, you can use a regular blender, but be careful of the hot steam and do not overfill the blender. Small batches are the safe way to go.
4. In a lightly oiled medium pan over medium heat, sauté the beets, leeks, carrots, canned tomatoes and tomato paste with the coconut sugar until the veggies are soft. Be careful not to overcook them or the beets will lose their color.
5. Combine the sautéed beet mixture with the soup base and cook for 2 minutes over medium heat. Do not let it boil.
6. Turn the heat off and stir in the dill, garlic, and salt and pepper to taste.

THE VEGAN CREAM OF ASPARAGUS SOUP

Asparagus contains the king of all antioxidants: glutathione! Glutathione recycles other antioxidants. It is a good source of inulin, a prebiotic important for a healthy colon. It's also packed with B vitamins, which are important for the proper digestion of carbohydrates and blood sugar regulation. For those of you who need a little more sleep, asparagus also supplies you with the sleep-inducing amino acid tryptophan.

Serves 4 • Prep time: 10 minutes

Total time: 30 minutes

Soup

1 bunch of fresh asparagus, hard ends cut off and the rest chopped into 1- to 2-inch pieces

3 cloves roasted garlic (optional)

1 can (13.5 oz) coconut milk (or ⅔ cup fresh young Thai coconut meat blended in the blender with 1 cup water)

1 tetra pack of vegetable broth (32 oz) or 4 cups water

2 Tbsp lemon juice

1 bay leaf

Sea salt to taste

Garnish

A pinch of pink salt (optional)

2–3 fresh tarragon leaves

Thumb-sized piece of freshly grated lemon rind

Freshly cracked pepper to taste

1. For the soup, place all ingredients in a saucepan and simmer for 20 minutes, until the asparagus is soft but still bright in color. Remove the bay leaf and discard it.
2. In batches, pour the soup into a blender and puree it, or use a hand-held immersion blender to puree it in the pot. If you are using a blender, be careful not to overfill it, and make sure you use a towel to hold the lid down as you blend—let's avoid a kitchen explosion.
3. Divide the soup into bowls and add the garnishes to taste.

THE CELERY ROOT AND LEEK CHOWDER

It's creamy, hearty, and satisfying. Most people aren't familiar with celeriac or celery root, but it has a creamy and earthy flavor that works beautifully in a soup. If you can't find it, add another head of cauliflower as a substitute.

Serves 10 • Prep time: 10 minutes
Total time: 60 minutes

8 cups water
1 celery root, peeled and cubed
1 head of cauliflower, cubed
4 leeks, white parts only, thinly sliced
4 cloves of garlic, crushed and chopped
1 tsp thyme
1 cup chopped parsley
2 Tbsp lemon juice
Fresh dill for garnish
Salt and pepper to taste

1. In a large soup pot over medium heat, add all ingredients except the parsley, lemon juice, dill, and salt and pepper.
2. Simmer for 30 minutes or until the celery root is tender.
3. Remove ¾ of the soup from the pot and puree in a blender (blend in small batches, being careful not to overfill the blender, and make sure you use a towel to hold the lid down as you blend).
4. Pour the pureed soup back into the pot and stir in the parsley and lemon juice. Serve with a garnish of dill and salt and pepper.

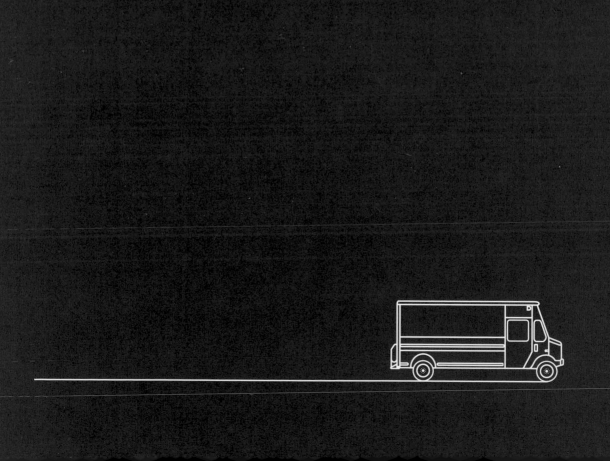

FINAL NOTES

ACKNOWLEDGEMENTS

We couldn't have made this cookbook without our Juice Truck team and our family.

Our team is everything. From our longtime friend and manager Lauren Ho (follow her amazing creations that pop up throughout the book at @fruitartbyloho), to our Chef Alina Bobylena, to our Production manager Fraser Lyons, and longtime Jack of All Trades man, Matt Petersen. The team from top to bottom is what makes work the incredibly positive space that it is. You guys are everything!

A special thanks to Meghan Parks for being the backbone behind most major projects and for always providing the support needed for whatever endeavor lies ahead.

Most importantly, I'd like to give gratitude to everyone that's ever supported our business over the past five years. Anyone that's ever come in for a juice or smoothie. You guys make it possible for us to continually pursue the work that we love. We're forever grateful. This would never be possible without all of you.

We're grateful to the Penguin Random House Canada team. Robert McCullough, for giving us this opportunity. Kiara Kent, for guiding us through the whole process. And to Elysse Bell and Paige Farrell, for supporting the project.

To our mentor Judy Brooks, thank you for always keeping us on the right path.

To Phoebe Glasfurd and Aren Fieldwalker (Glasfurd & Walker Design) for creating what we envisioned for The Juice Truck back in 2010.

To Alison Page, Brian Van Wyk, and Juno Kim for creating photography in such a playful, lively manner. And to Jessica Robson for everything that you do too.

To our Vancouver small business support team: Aly Maz, Jian Pablico, Keighty Gallagher, Dallah El Chami, Erin Ireland, and Christina Culver.

A huge thank you to our family. Our Moms, Dads, brothers, and sisters. We love you guys. We're thankful for your endless support and love.

To all of the pioneers in plant-based eating. For inspiring us and leading the way for personal and environmental balance.

And lastly, our love goes to Eden MacDonald. You will forever inspire us to continue down this path of love, health, and wellness.

INDEX

Appetite by Random House® and colophon are registered trademarks of Penguin Random House LLC.

Library and Archives of Canada Cataloguing in Publication is available upon request.
ISBN: 978-0-14-753001-1
eBook ISBN: 978-0-14-753002-8

Brand created by Glasfurd & Walker Design
Book creative direction by Glasfurd & Walker Design
Photography provided by Anita Cheung,
Tigh Farley, Alison Page, Juno Kim, Jason Scott,
Brian Van Wyk, Jeremy Jude Lee, Abdallah El Chami,
Thompson Chan, and Sophia Hsin.

Printed and bound in China

Published in Canada by Appetite by Random House®, a division of Penguin Random House Canada Limited.

www.penguinrandomhouse.ca

10 9 8 7 6 5 4 3 2 1

appetite
by RANDOM HOUSE

Penguin
Random
House